The Messiah's Baptism

Moving Beyond the Ritual Washing

The Messiah's Baptism

Moving Beyond
the Ritual Washing

T. Alex Tennent

Messianic Publishing LLC

Copyright © 2018 by T. Alex Tennent

All rights reserved. No part of this publication may be reproduced, stored in a retrieval system, or transmitted, in any form or by any means, electronic, mechanical, photocopying, recording, or otherwise, without the prior written permission of the author.

Front cover design by Abdul Wahid and Mi Ae Lipe.
Interior text design by Mi Ae Lipe, What Now Design.

For an electronically searchable version of this book,
an ebook is available.
To contact the author or order additional print copies or ebooks:
TheMessiahsBaptism.com

Also, see the author's other book at
TheMessianicFeast.com

Print edition ISBN: 978-0-9897656-3-3
E-book edition ISBN: 978-1-5456332-4-3
Library of Congress: 2017917418

*This book is dedicated to all those
who esteem the word of God
higher than the traditions of men.*

Table of Contents

ACKNOWLEDGMENTS | ix

A NOTE TO READERS | x

INTRODUCTION | xi

1. **WHAT BAPTISM IS AND ITS SIGNIFICANCE FOR MOST BELIEVERS** | 1

2. **WHY CHRISTIANS MUST UNDERSTAND THE JEWISH BAPTISMS** | 4
   - 2.1 | 5 — The First Baptism: Elisha Tells Naaman to Go "Wash"
   - 2.2 | 8 — Then Came John the "Washer"
   - 2.3 | 10 — The Baptism (Ritual Washing) of John
   - 2.4 | 12 — Baptism before Approaching God, as in the Temple
   - 2.5 | 13 — Their Ritual Baths for Cleansing Were Also Called Baptisms
   - 2.6 | 15 — The Jewish *Mikveh* for Ritual Baptisms
   - 2.7 | 17 — These Water Baptisms Also Required for Gentile Proselytes

3. **THE MESSIAH'S SPIRIT BAPTISM SUPERSEDES JOHN'S WATER BAPTISM** | 21
   - 3.1 | 21 — The Messiah Wanted His Holy Spirit Baptism Brought Forth, but…
   - 3.2 | 24 — Living Waters Were for Ritual Washings until the Messiah's Baptism
   - 3.3 | 27 — Ritual Washings in Water until the Resurrection and New Order
   - 3.4 | 29 — Spiritually Washed with the Messiah's Baptism
   - 3.5 | 31 — Baptize/Wash All Nations in Water?
   - 3.6 | 33 — Baptism "in the Name of" and How Rome Misinterpreted It
   - 3.7 | 35 — What Exactly Did "in the Name of" Mean in the Jewish Idiom?

4. **HOW THE NATURAL-TO-SPIRITUAL IDIOM AMONG THE JEWS EXPLAINS MANY BAPTISM SCRIPTURES** | 41
   - 4.1 | 42 — They Were Now in the Promised New Covenant

4.2	44	Spiritual Truth and Parables
4.3	46	Old Covenant Events, Sacrifices, and Services All Point Forward

5. SPIRITUALLY WASHED, NOT BAPTIZED IN WATER | 51

5.1	51	New Covenant: Were They Baptized/Washed in Water, or Spiritually Washed/Baptized?
5.2	53	Baptize/Wash in the Natural-to-Spiritual Idiom
5.3	57	Viewing Certain Scriptures through the Proper Lens
5.4	59	Early Messianic Jews Dispute the Roman Baptism
5.5	61	Cleaning/Washing the Outside of the Cup

6. A CLOSER LOOK: WHY DID PAUL SAY CHRIST DID NOT SEND ME TO BAPTIZE? | 68

6.1	68	At the Heart: 1 Corinthians
6.2	71	The Commentators Weigh In on Paul's Words
6.3	74	What the Commentators Say about Verses 16 and 17
6.4	78	Analyzing Hebrews 9:10
6.5	82	The Influence of Tertullian and the Jewish Disconnect

7. A CLOSER LOOK: BUT PETER SAID BAPTISM SAVES YOU | 86

7.1	87	Peter and the "Washing" That Saves Us
7.2	88	Reasons Why Peter Does Not Mean That Baptism *in Water* Saves Us
7.3	91	The Simple Answer for 1 Peter 3:21
7.4	93	More on Why Peter Mentions Noah

8. THE EXCELLENT BENEFITS OF THE HOLY SPIRIT INFILLING | 97

8.1	97	The Messiah's Holy Spirit Baptism and the Holy Spirit Infilling
8.2	101	The Holy Spirit Quenches Our Spiritual Thirst
8.3	102	The Holy Spirit Brings Joy, Comfort, and Rest
8.4	103	God's Holy Spirit Will Lead and Teach Us
8.5	105	Speaking in Tongues Is the Sign of Receiving
8.6	108	Why Speak in Tongues?
8.7	110	The Holy Spirit Is Needed to Prepare the Spiritual Bride

9. SOME ADDITIONAL BAPTISM SCRIPTURES EXPLAINED | 112

9.1 | 112   List of Twelve Reasons against Water Baptism in the New Covenant
9.2 | 116   Matthew 3:13–17: Why Was Jesus Water Baptized?
9.3 | 118   John 3: Born Again, and the Supposed Baptismal Regeneration
9.4 | 121   John 3:22–23 and John 4:1: The Disciples of Christ Water Baptizing
9.5 | 122   Water Baptisms in the Book of Acts: A Time of Transition
9.6 | 125   Acts 2: The Promise of the Father
9.7 | 129   Acts 8:12–17: Those in Samaria Are Washed/Baptized by Believing
9.8 | 131   Acts 8:38: The Water Baptism of the Eunuch
9.9 | 132   Acts 9 and 22: The Supposed Water Baptism of Paul
9.10 | 135   Acts 16:13–15: The Baptism/Washing of Lydia and her Household
9.11 | 136   Acts 16:30–33: The Prison Baptism/Washing Stumps the Commentators
9.12 | 139   Acts 19:1–7: The Baptism/Washing in Ephesus
9.13 | 142   Acts 22:16
9.14 | 142   1 Corinthians 15:29: Baptized for the Dead Ones
9.15 | 144   Romans 6:3–5, Galatians 3:27, and Colossians 2:12: Baptized into the Messiah's Death
9.16 | 147   Hebrews 6:1–2: Moving Beyond the Teaching on Baptisms/Washings
9.17 | 149   Conclusion of the Matter

10. QUESTIONS AND ANSWERS | 150

INDEX OF BAPTISM SCRIPTURES | 155
BIBLIOGRAPHY | 162
PERMISSIONS | 164

Acknowledgments

I want to thank my editor Mi Ae Lipe for her excellent work in shaping this manuscript into its present form. Additional thanks to all the reviewers, and special thanks to my wife Patricia, Rich Kelsey, and John and Mary Catherine Koppang, who offered helpful insight and raised important points that changed the book for the better.

A Note to Readers

This book has several typographical conventions that deserve clarification. In quoted material (from scripture or other sources), I have sometimes added boldface for emphasis. In quoted scripture, italicized text is part of that particular translation of the Bible, usually indicating that a particular word or phrase was not in the original Greek or Hebrew text but has been added to the English edition by the translators. The italicized words are part of the translation and have not been added or altered by me except when otherwise noted.

In this book, I have sometimes quoted only fragments of scriptures and other material and not entire sentences for the sake of brevity and context. Sometimes these scriptures end with a comma, semicolon, or no ending punctuation at all. I have chosen to keep the punctuation (or lack of it) as it was in the original source, especially in the case of scripture, so as not to jeopardize nuances in meaning or introduce distraction. While these may look like errors at times when scriptures end with a comma or semicolon, my intent was to preserve the exact translation in each scripture. With longer quotations, I have indicated omissions with the ellipses (…) at the beginning or end of the paragraph where appropriate.

Introduction

"Prove all things; hold fast that which is good."

— KJV 1 Thessalonians 5:21 —

The teaching that water baptism is required by the Lord for all believers is almost universal throughout various Christian denominations. We see in the scriptures that the Messiah told the apostles to baptize all nations, and we sometimes see the apostles themselves connected to water baptism; therefore, almost all believe it is a rite we must keep.

Certain technical aspects are debated as to how this act should be performed (sprinkle, immerse, pour), what phrase should be spoken over the one being baptized ("I now baptize you in the name of Jesus" or "I now baptize you in the name of the Father, the Son, and the Holy Spirit"), how old one should be before being baptized, whether it is necessary for salvation, and other such points of contention.

While these doctrinal differences are often discussed, what is almost never questioned is the act of water baptism itself. However, since we are commanded in the scripture above to "prove all things," I will attempt to prove in this book that the Lord did not intend water baptism in the New Covenant. Instead, believers should be baptized with the Holy Spirit, not with water.

Since the ritual of water baptism itself is almost universally accepted among all believers, you may wonder why this is even relevant now. Why spend time reading a book with the premise that the Messiah does not want this rite for us today? To answer this question, this introduction will offer a few scriptural points as appetizers, in the hope that the reader will consider and weigh the complete proofs shown later in this book.

And if all of this focus on water baptism has actually caused churches to miss the real baptism the Messiah wanted—the Spirit baptism—then that is another reason to carefully weigh and consider the facts that this book brings out.

The Roman Catholic Church is known for having seven sacraments. A sacrament is a word adopted by the Latin Church for an ordinance of religion that is a sign that points to what is sacred and important for all Catholics. Obedience to the sacraments is said to bring about favor from God. Yet, when the Protestants left the Catholic Church, they dropped five of these seven sacraments—Confirmation, Penance, Orders, Matrimony, and Extreme Unction.

Of the remaining two sacraments, my first book, *The Messianic Feast: Moving Beyond the Ritual*, proved that the ritual of Communion (also called the Blessed Eucharist) as kept by most churches is a sixth sacramental rite that did not come from the Lord and therefore should have also been dropped. In this book on baptism, we question the seventh (and now only remaining) sacrament, water baptism.

The baptism that the Messiah said he would bring was the Holy Spirit baptism (in God's Spirit), and it clearly contrasts with the water baptisms (ritual immersions) that the Jews were familiar with under the Old Covenant.

The scriptures declare that God sent John the Baptist to baptize the Israelites in water. John was a prophet, and the majority of people in Israel held him in that high esteem. Both John and Jesus contrasted John's *water baptism* with the future *Spirit baptism* the Messiah would bring, emphasizing how different the latter would be.

Notice how John contrasts this, specifically using the word "**but**" as he spoke multiple times below:

> [NAS] Mark 1:8 "I baptized you with water; **but** He will baptize you with the Holy Spirit."

> [NAS] Matthew 3:11 "As for me, I baptize you with water for repentance, **but** He who is coming after me is mightier than I, and I am not fit to remove His sandals; He will baptize you with the Holy Spirit and fire.

> NAS John 1:33 "And I did not recognize Him, **but He who sent me to baptize in water** said to me, 'He upon whom you see the Spirit descending and remaining upon Him, this is the one who **baptizes in the Holy Spirit**.'"

And Jesus himself consistently shows this same contrast using the same word:

> NAS Acts 1:5 for John baptized with water, **but** you shall be baptized with the Holy Spirit not many days from now."

And the apostle Peter, speaking right after God filled the uncircumcised Gentiles with the Holy Spirit, remembered that the Lord used to tell them about this contrast of baptisms:

> NAS Acts 11:16 "And I remembered the word of the Lord, **how He used to say**, 'John baptized with water, **but** you shall be baptized with the Holy Spirit.'"

None of the scriptures say "John baptized in water **and** the Messiah will add the baptism in the Holy Spirit so that we will now have two baptisms." The contrasting "but" in every verse is a sure clue that under the Messiah (and now in the promised New Covenant), we will move away from water baptism and forward to Holy Spirit baptism. We will explore this further in later chapters with abundant proofs, but for now, let it be said that Jesus himself never baptized anyone in water.

> NAS John 3:22 After these things Jesus and His disciples came into the land of Judea, and there He was spending time with them and baptizing.

Since this verse occurred while still in the time of the Old Covenant, where ritual water immersion was required for entering the Temple, disciples were baptizing in water (ritually immersing), but the scripture specifically states that Jesus was not:

> ^{NAS} John 4:2 (although Jesus Himself was not baptizing, but His disciples were),

Later on, after the Resurrection and now under the New Covenant, Paul actually thanks God that he baptized only a few people and states very emphatically that Christ did not send him to baptize:

> ^{NAS} 1 Corinthians 1:14 **I thank God** that I baptized none of you except Crispus and Gaius,

> ^{NAS} 1 Corinthians 1:17 For **Christ did not send me to baptize**, but to preach the gospel, not in cleverness of speech, that the cross of Christ should not be made void.

Why would Jesus not baptize people in water (John 4:2 further above) if this was something God wanted **him** to do? And why did Paul first baptize a few and then change his mind and stop water baptizing, even thanking God he had baptized so few and saying it was because Christ did not send him to baptize?

The answer to the question concerning Jesus is that he knew what God's will was, and that God was not leading him to baptize people in water. As for Paul, he was at first going along with the flow of the first-century Jewish ritual immersions in water, so he baptized a couple of people this way. But once he realized that the Messiah was not calling him to continue the Old Covenant baptisms in water, he thanked God for this new understanding and ceased from carrying out the ritual water immersions.

This introduction offers a small glimpse into the points I will cover in subsequent chapters. History makes clear that Rome changed certain aspects of baptism. The point of focus became water baptism instead of the Messiah's Spirit baptism because the Roman Church's regulations over who got to be water baptized gave it great power over the people, even over kings. And with Rome being the world power of that period, these erroneous teachings have been handed down for generations.

One main distinction with this baptism book is that it will explore baptism scriptures from within first-century Jewish idioms instead of from the traditional Roman perspective, and it will consider if important truth was lost in what has been handed down ever since. By keeping an open mind and being ready to interpret the scriptures as they were originally intended, you will hopefully find that this book forever expands and enlightens your view of baptism.

1

What Baptism Is
and Its Significance for Most Believers

The actual Greek words translated as "baptize" (*baptizo*) and "baptism" (*baptisma*) in English translations mean to immerse or wash.

Most people today have at least some concept of what water baptism is. However, far fewer know what baptism meant to first-century Jews at the time when Jesus and John the Baptist ministered. To understand the difference between Jewish baptism and what baptism became in the Roman Catholic Church (and later with the Protestants), let's first consider the meanings given in their respective religious encyclopedias.

From *The Jewish Encyclopedia* (boldface my own for emphasis):

> **BAPTISM**
> A religious ablution signifying purification or consecration. The natural method of cleansing the body by washing and bathing in water was always customary in Israel (see Ablution, Bathing). The washing of their clothes was an important means of sanctification enjoined on the Israelites before the Revelation on Mt. Sinai (Ex. xix. 10). The Rabbis connect with this the duty of bathing by complete immersion ("ṭebilah," Yeb. 46*b*; Mek., Baḥodesh, iii.); and since sprinkling with blood was always accompanied by immersion, tradition connects with this immersion the blood lustration mentioned as having also taken place immediately before the Revelation (Ex. xxiv. 8), these three acts being the initiatory rites **always performed upon proselytes**, "to bring them under the wings of the Shekinah" (Yeb. *l.c.*).[1]

---

1 *The Jewish Encyclopedia*, vol. 2, p. 499, s.v. "Baptism."

And baptism explained from *The Catholic Encyclopedia*:

> **BAPTISM**
> One of the Seven Sacraments of the Christian Church, frequently called the "first sacrament," the "door of the sacraments," and the "door of the Church." [2]

And this with the prescribed words:

> **DEFINITION**
> The Roman Catechism (Ad parochos, De bapt., 2, 2, 5) defines baptism thus: Baptism is the sacrament of regeneration by water in the word (*per aquam in verbo*). St. Thomas Aquinas (III, Q. lxvi, a. 1) gives this definition: "Baptism is the external ablution of the body, **performed with the prescribed form of words.**" [3]

Notice that the Catholic definition of baptism added something that the Jewish baptism did not contain—that Christian baptism was to be "performed with the prescribed form of words."

In this book, I will explain how the Roman Catholic-Christian concept of saying a prescribed set of words during a baptism originated from a misunderstanding of first-century Jewish idioms. And this in turn led to the misinterpretation of certain scriptures.

Rome's belief on the prescribed words for baptism also came from a literal interpretation of "in the name of" in the following scripture:

> NAS Matthew 28:19 "Go therefore and make disciples of all the nations, baptizing them **in the name of** the Father and the Son and the Holy Spirit,

---

2   Herbermann et al, *The Catholic Encyclopedia*, vol. 2, p. 258, s.v. "Baptism."
3   Herbermann et al, *The Catholic Encyclopedia*, vol. 2, p. 259, s.v. "Baptism."

We see something similar in the following verse, which says to do essentially everything in the name of Jesus; yet, it is not referring to a prescribed set of words that must be used before each thing one does:

> ^{NAS} Colossians 3:17   And **whatever you do** in word or deed, ***do* all in the name of the Lord Jesus**, giving thanks through Him to God the Father.

This scripture telling us that whatever we do, we are to do all "in the name of the Lord Jesus," meant one thing in the Jewish idiom, but, concerning Matthew 28:19, an entirely different thing in the Catholic belief that came later. When Paul, speaking from the Jewish idiom, said to do "all in the name of" the Lord Jesus, he did not mean that when you brush your teeth, you are to now say a prescribed form of the words "I now brush my teeth in the name of Jesus." Nor does it mean that every time you to go to church or to the store, you say "I now go to church and to the store in the name of the Lord Jesus."

This was also not what was meant when the scriptures speak of baptism "**in the name of** the Father, the Son, and the Holy Spirit" (the Roman Catholic prescribed formula), or the baptism "**in the name** of Jesus" (the mostly Protestant formula).

As the next two chapters of this book further examine first-century Jewish baptisms, it will become clear that water baptism with its prescribed formula of words was not what the Messiah intended. In fact, he wanted believers to move forward to *his* baptism—Spirit baptism.

2

Why Christians Must Understand the Jewish Baptisms

When many Christians hear the word "baptism," they picture only the Christian rite, and they do not think of baptism as an already existing part of Jewish history. But in fact, Jewish ceremonial cleansings with water (which Jews themselves called baptisms, using the same Greek word for baptism) existed long before Jesus or John the Baptist ministered. Many do not realize that these baptisms played an integral role in Jewish life for centuries before Christ's time.

This chapter will examine this full Jewish history, from the prophet Elisha telling the leprous Naaman to go "wash" in the Jordan, to God's instructions to wash before entering His presence, as well as the *mikveh* baths for ritual baptisms that have been excavated all around Jerusalem. This knowledge will help set the stage for understanding the Messiah's baptism and the way the Greek word for baptism was used among the Jews. And to properly comprehend many scriptures on baptism and what baptism meant to Jesus, Paul, John the Baptist, and the other Jewish disciples, we must understand its importance to Jews before they ministered.

It is also imperative to understand that when first-century Jews spoke of baptism, one must not immediately think of the Roman Catholic baptism that has been handed down, because the Roman church did not yet exist when Jesus lived. Instead, we must understand how this word "baptism" was used by both Old Covenant and New Covenant Jews.

In Jewish history and in how this word was used, the most important meaning that carries forward into the New Testament scriptures is "washed." When we view this meaning through the first-century Jewish idioms in which the scriptures were written, we will see how the New

Testament Jewish understanding of baptism was quite different from what has been handed down since the Church in Rome gained control.

2.1 THE FIRST BAPTISM: ELISHA TELLS NAAMAN TO GO "WASH"

Most Christians today would not equate the instance of Elisha telling the leper Naaman to go wash in the Jordan seven times with a Christian baptism (2 Kings 5:1–14). In fact, the word "baptism" is found nowhere in the Hebrew Old Testament, but this is because baptism was not a Hebrew but a Greek word. However, when Jewish scholars translated the Hebrew Old Testament into Greek, they did use the word "baptism" for the washing that Naaman did. (The resulting document was the Septuagint, which was translated about 200 years before John the Baptist ministered.)

In fact, Jewish scholars not only equate baptism to Naaman dipping seven times in the Jordan, but also to Elisha pouring water on Elijah's hands, which they see as another ritual washing in water, as *The Jewish Encyclopedia* mentions under the subject of baptism:

> **BAPTISM**
> …The real significance of the rite of **Baptism** can not be derived from the Levitical law; but it appears to have had its origin in Babylonian or ancient Semitic practise. As it was the special service administered by Elisha, as prophetic disciple to Elijah his master, to "**pour out water** upon his hands" (II Kings iii. 11), so did Elisha tell Naaman **to bathe** seven times in the Jordan, in order to recover from his leprosy (II Kings v. 10).[4]

So we see that baptism among the Jews was different from the Christian baptism that has been handed down from Rome, wherein the latter a certain prescribed formula is spoken over people as they are baptized in water. Accurate history shows that Jews practiced these various forms of ritual cleansing and that they were called baptisms (using the Greek

---

4 *The Jewish Encyclopedia*, vol. 2, p. 500, s.v. "Baptism."

words for baptize and baptism) for hundreds of years before Jesus or John the Baptist. When Elisha told Naaman to go "wash" in the Jordan river, the Greek word for what Naaman then did (as written in the Septuagint) is "baptized," declaring that Naaman baptized himself seven times (2 Kings 5:10–14).

> NAS 2 Kings 5:10 And Elisha sent a messenger to him, saying, "Go and **wash** in the Jordan seven times, and your flesh shall be restored to you and *you shall* be clean."

> NAS 2 Kings 5:14 So he went down and **dipped**[5] *himself* seven times in the Jordan, according to the word of the man of God; and his flesh was restored like the flesh of a little child, and he was clean.

The Septuagint was the common bible in Christ's day, and the majority of Old Testament scripture quotes in the New Testament come from this translation. So this word for baptism used here where Elisha had told Naaman to go "**wash**" would have been very common among first-century Jews. And as we will see from all Jewish history, the words "wash" and "baptism" are closely intertwined in their idiom, a point that is vitally important when understanding certain scriptures correctly.

When *The Jewish Encyclopedia* above mentions the scripture where Elisha pours water on the prophet Elijah's hands and connects this to baptism, this explains another New Testament scripture that is often obscured by translators. When translated correctly, this scripture below shows this connection between Jewish history and this word "baptism" and how the Jewish nation connected it to their ritual cleansings.

Young's Literal Translation does a better job translating the actual Greek words Mark used here, and you can see below that in Jewish history, this Greek word for baptism was regularly used for their ritual washings before Jesus and John the Baptist ministered:

---

5   The Greek word translated as "dipped" above is the Greek word for baptized in the Septuagint.

2. Why Christians Must Understand the Jewish Baptisms

> ^{YLT} Mark 7:3   for the Pharisees, and all the Jews, if they do not **wash the hands to the wrist**, do not eat, holding the tradition of the elders,
>
> ^{YLT} Mark 7:4   and, *coming* from the market-place, if they do not **baptize themselves**, they do not eat; and many other things there are that they received to hold, **baptisms** of cups, and pots, and brazen vessels, and couches. [6]

The "baptize themselves" in verse 4 refers directly back to the "wash the hands to the wrist" in verse 3. You can see how an accurate translation of the Greek gives extra meaning and understanding to why *The Jewish Encyclopedia* used "baptism" to refer to Elisha pouring out water on the hands of Elijah in its earlier quote.

Almost all other English translations leave out the words "wash their hands to the wrist," plus the Greek word for baptism is translated as "washing" or "wash" in this scripture because the translators probably did not want to connect the Jewish ceremonial washings to the Christian rite of baptism. For instance, here is the King James translation of these scriptures:

> ^{KJV} Mark 7:2   And when they saw some of his disciples eat bread with defiled, that is to say, with unwashen, hands, they found fault. For the Pharisees, and all the Jews, **except they wash *their* hands oft**, eat not, holding the tradition of the elders. And *when they come* from the market, except they **wash**, they eat not. And many other things there be, which they have received to hold, *as* the **washing** of cups, and pots, brasen vessels, and of tables. Then the Pharisees and scribes asked him, Why walk not thy disciples according to the tradition of the elders, but eat bread with unwashen hands?

The translators probably felt that these Jewish baptisms did not equate with the Christian baptism that has been handed down from Rome, so

---

[6]   The Greek word for couches above means "stretcher" or "sick bed."

they must be pictured and translated as something else. But to properly understand baptism in the New Testament scriptures, it is essential to see what this word truly meant in the idiom of these Jewish writers.

Washing the hands before eating bread was a ritual cleansing for purification that was a tradition of the Pharisees (the full history on this and how it came about, beginning from the high order of priests washing before partaking of the Showbread in the Temple, is covered in my first book, *The Messianic Feast*, in Course 3, titled "The Jewish Idiom of Breaking Bread Among the Early Believers." That chapter and many others can be found online at http://themessianicfeast.com/sample-chapters/).

2.2 THEN CAME JOHN THE "WASHER"

As we have just seen, prior to John the Baptist's ministry, the Jews already had a clear concept of baptizing (washing) for ritual purity.

John the Baptist said that God called him to baptize in water to prepare the people for a visitation of the Lord (John 1:31; Luke 1:17, 23). So this is right in line with the long Jewish history that came before John's baptism, where a washing was required before certain events, such as when entering God's presence (more on this in the next section).

When the Pharisees sent priests from Jerusalem to first inquire with John the Baptist about his authority to baptize (John 1:19–24), it was clear that they understood from the scriptures that it was the Messiah who would come to baptize (wash) the people.

> ^{NAS}John 1:24–25 Now they had been sent from the Pharisees. And they asked him, and said to him, "**Why then are you baptizing**, if you are not the **Christ**, nor **Elijah**, nor the **Prophet**?"

These Jewish scholars believed that the coming Messiah would be the one who would come and wash/baptize the people and not anyone else (like John), so that is why they were asking John what he was doing baptizing since he was not the Christ. Also, it is worth noting that when these men who were sent from the Pharisees mention Christ, the Prophet, and Elijah, they are referring to the same individual, for "the Prophet" referred to the Messiah that Moses had foretold (Deuteronomy 18:15), and some also believed that the Messiah would be Elijah returned. So, in reality, their question concerned the same person.

This understanding of the anointed one coming to wash/baptize most likely came from the following scriptures in Malachi (the last Jewish prophet before John the Baptist). Below, the coming "messenger" would wash the people with "fullers' soap" (the strongest soap known), and Malachi connected this to Elijah, who was to come:

> NAS Malachi 3:1–2 "Behold, I am going to send **My messenger**, and he will clear the way before Me. And the Lord, whom you seek, will suddenly come to His temple; and the messenger of the covenant, in whom you delight, behold, He is coming," says the LORD of hosts. "But who can endure the day of His coming? And who can stand when He appears? For He is like a refiner's fire and **like fullers' soap**.

> NAS Malachi 4:5 "Behold, I am going to send you **Elijah the prophet** before the coming of the great and terrible day of the LORD.

However, Jesus explained that this messenger who would wash the people and thus prepare the way for a manifestation of God's presence was really John the Baptist, as he speaks of John here:

> NAS Matthew 11:10 "This is the one about whom it is written, 'Behold, **I send My messenger** before Your face, **Who will prepare** Your way before You.'

And the prophecy extended to the Messiah as well, who would baptize (wash) in the Holy Spirit. And consider Malachi 3:3, where silver is purified and refined in the fire:

> NAS Malachi 3:3 "And He will sit as a smelter and purifier of silver, and He will purify the sons of Levi and refine them like gold and silver, so that they may present to the LORD offerings in righteousness.

And as for this refiner's fire (Malachi 3:2, further above), John said:

> NAS Luke 3:16 John answered and said to them all, "As for me, **I baptize you with water; but** One is coming who is mightier than I, and I am not fit to untie the thong of His sandals; **He will baptize** you with the Holy Spirit **and fire.**

These scholarly Jews understood the scriptural promise that the messenger, who they thought would be the Messiah, would come and wash (baptize) the people (as with fullers' soap) in preparation of the Lord (i.e., Yahweh). That is what those scriptures in Malachi implied. The fullers' soap did not mean that this "messenger" (John) would literally scrub each one with soap but was referring only to the depth of the washing; it was a thorough *ritual* washing to prepare for a visitation from God. It was not an actual scrubbing of the body to remove dirt but a purifying ritual.

And this is why the Pharisees had sent men asking John if he was Elijah (or the Christ) and if not, why then was he baptizing.

2.3 THE BAPTISM (RITUAL WASHING) OF JOHN

One must understand the washings/baptisms that the Jews did for purification to ascertain what this word meant in the first-century Jewish mind, before any influence Christ or John the Baptist may have had entered the picture.

> NAS John 11:55 Now the Passover of the Jews was at hand, and many went up to Jerusalem out of the country **before the Passover, to purify themselves.**

We saw that Jewish people before the first century had various ceremonial cleansings with water (called baptism, bathing, washing, etc.). This existing familiarity with water baptism is part of why John the Baptist and his water baptisms were so easily accepted by the Jewish people—it was not some new, unheard-of process.

> NAS Matthew 3:4–6 Now John himself had a garment of camel's hair, and a leather belt about his waist; and his food was locusts and wild honey. Then **Jerusalem was going out to him, and all Judea, and all the district around the Jordan**; and they were being **baptized** by him in the Jordan River, as they confessed their sins.

Jewish scholars understood that the baptisms John carried out connected directly to their history of various ritual "washings"; we see this here when *The Jewish Encyclopedia* quotes the famous first-century Jewish historian Josephus:

> Accordingly, **Baptism** is not merely for the purpose of expiating a special transgression, as is the case chiefly in the violation of the so-called Levitical laws of purity; but it is to form a part of holy living and to prepare for the attainment of a closer communion with God. This thought is expressed in the well-known passage in Josephus in which he speaks of John the Baptist ("Ant." xviii. 5, § 2): "The **washing** would be acceptable to him, if they made use of it, not in order to the putting away of some sins, but for the purification of the body; supposing still that the soul was thoroughly purified beforehand by righteousness."[7]

This explanation sheds light on why the Jewish prophet John the Baptist would rebuke certain Pharisees and Sadducees who were coming to his baptism-washing (Matthew 3:7); it was because he knew their hearts were not "thoroughly purified beforehand by righteousness."

---

7   *The Jewish Encyclopedia*, vol. 2, p. 499, s.v. "Baptism."

And of course John the Baptist was ministering to Jewish people, not Gentiles. There were no people called "Christians" when John lived; when he first appeared on the scene in Israel, he was baptizing Jews, who had mostly not yet heard of Jesus. But just as Jews would wash in water before approaching God in the Temple, so did God send John to baptize/wash the people to ritually prepare them for His coming presence that would indwell the Messiah.

2.4 BAPTISM BEFORE APPROACHING GOD, AS IN THE TEMPLE

In this time in Jewish history, it was very clearly understood that when one was entering God's presence, whether first with Moses (Exodus 30:20) or later at the Temple in Jerusalem, a strict requirement was to first be washed in water (baptized, bathed) before entering. It was well-known from the experiences and teachings of Moses that one would never want to appear before God in an unclean or unwashed state, for God is holy.

The famous rabbinic scholar Moses Maimonides wrote in *The Guide for the Perplexed* about how even those who were clean had to first take the ritual bath in water (i.e., baptism) before entering the Temple precincts:

> Moses Maimonides:
>
> Life of Maimonides Morch Nebuchim Literature. Analysis of the Guide for the Perplexed:
>
> Our Sages, **as is well known**, said, "Even a clean person may not enter the Sanctuary for the purpose of performing divine service, **unless he takes previously a bath**." By such acts the reverence [for the Sanctuary] will continue, the right impression will be produced which leads man, as is intended, to humility.[8]

---

8 Maimonides, *The Guide for the Perplexed*, Part 3, ch. 47, pp. 367–368, http://www.sacred-texts.com/jud/gfp/gfp183.htm.

And first-century Jewish philosopher Philo echoes the same understanding:

> It is necessary, therefore, for those **who are about to go into the temple** to partake of the sacrifice, **to be cleansed as to their bodies** and as to their souls before their bodies.⁹

2.5 THEIR RITUAL BATHS FOR CLEANSING WERE ALSO CALLED BAPTISMS

Jewish history makes it clear that water baptisms (ceremonial cleansings with water) were common in Israel long before Jesus or John the Baptist, as *The Jewish Encyclopedia* indicates under its baptism definition:

> BAPTISM: A religious ablution signifying purification or consecration. The natural method of **cleansing** the body by **washing and bathing in water was always customary** among the Israelites (**see Bathing**).¹⁰

The focus of these baptisms was not just on outward cleanness, because there was also an inward ritual cleansing that was pictured—a sense of being cleansed and right with God. We repeatedly see in the Jewish idiom that baptism to Jews is the same as the baths and ceremonial washings that were often commanded by God in the Law of Moses. Here are just a few examples:

> ᴺᴬˢ Exodus 30:20   when they enter the tent of meeting, they shall **wash with water**, that they may not die; or when they approach the altar to minister, by offering up in smoke a fire *sacrifice* to the LORD.

---

9   Yonge, *The Works of Philo Judaeus*, "Special Laws I," 50:269, http://www.earlyjewishwritings.com/text/philo/book27.html.

10   *The Jewish Encyclopedia*, vol. 2, p. 499, s.v. "Baptism."

^{NAS} Leviticus 14:8 "The one to be cleansed shall then wash his clothes and shave off all his hair, **and bathe in water and be clean**. Now afterward, he may enter the camp, but he shall stay outside his tent for seven days.

^{NAS} Numbers 19:19 "Then the clean *person* shall sprinkle on the unclean on the third day and on the seventh day; and on the seventh day he shall **purify him from uncleanness**, and he shall wash his clothes **and bathe *himself* in water and shall be clean by evening**.

The following two quotes from *The Jewish Encyclopedia* under the Baptism entry also show the importance of this ritual washing in their idiom:

> **The original form of Baptism—frequent bathing in cold water**—remained in use later among the sects that had a somewhat Jewish character, such as the Ebionites, Baptists, and Hemerobaptists (compare Ber. iii. 6); and at the present day the Sabeans and Mandeans deem frequent bathing a duty (compare Sibyllines, iv. 164, in which, even in Christian times, the heathens are invited to bathe in streams).

And this:

> To receive the spirit of God, or to be permitted to stand in the presence of God (His Shekinah), man **must undergo Baptism** (Tan., Meẓora', 6, ed. Buber, p. 46), wherefore **in the Messianic time God will Himself pour water of purification** upon Israel in accordance with Ezek. xxxvi. 25 (Tan., Meẓora', 9–17, 18, ed. Buber, pp. 43, 53).[11]

---

11   *The Jewish Encyclopedia*, vol. 2, p. 499, s.v. "Baptism."

2. WHY CHRISTIANS MUST UNDERSTAND THE JEWISH BAPTISMS

So as we come down to the time when Jesus and John the Baptist ministered, these various shades of meaning with this Greek word for baptism (from within their idiom) must be understood.

2.6 THE JEWISH *MIKVEH* FOR RITUAL BAPTISMS

The requirement of the ritual bath (baptism) before entering the Temple explains why so many *mikvehs*, or stone enclosure–type bathing areas, have been found in archaeological digs near the Temple location in Jerusalem. And this immersion in water in the *mikveh* (also spelled *mikweh*, *mikvah*) was of vital importance to the first-century Jew, especially before entering the Temple.

The Hebrew word for *mikveh* (*miqra*) refers to a gathering or collection, and in connection to baptism refers to a collection of water. *The Jewish Encyclopedia* states how this word became connected with ritual purification:

> Because of the use made of this word in connection with **ritual** purification (Lev. xi. 36), it has become the term commonly used to designate the **ritual bath. In all cases of ritual impurity it was necessary for the person or object to be immersed** in a bath built in accordance with the rules laid down by the Rabbis (see Ablution; Baths; Purity).[12]

And this:

> The **ritual bath** always formed one of the most important institutions of a Jewish community (see Abrahams, "Jewish Life in the Middle Ages," p. 73).[13]

The Jewish Virtual Library explains that these ritual baths have been found in large numbers around Jerusalem, where the Temple was located:

---

12 *The Jewish Encyclopedia*, vol. 8, p. 588, s.v. "Mikweh."
13 *The Jewish Encyclopedia*, vol. 8, p. 588, s.v. "Mikweh."

During the Second Temple period (roughly from 100 B.C.E. to 70 C.E.), the Jewish population in Palestine had a very distinctive practice of purification within water installations known as *mikva'ot*. Large numbers of stepped-and-plastered *mikva'ot* have been found in excavations in Jerusalem, in outlying villages, as well as at various rural locations.[14]

For certain ritual cleansings, God had specified running or "living waters," as we will see in the next chapter:

> The water of the miḳweh must come from a natural spring or from a river that has its source in a natural spring (Sifra to Lev. xi. 36).[15]

Another important aspect concerning the baptisms and baths in the *mikvehs* is that they were not primarily intended as physical washings but spiritual cleansings, as *Encyclopedia Judaica* declares:

> It is emphasized that the purpose of immersion is not physical, but spiritual, cleanliness.[16]

So critical was their function that the *mikvehs* were surprisingly large—enough to completely immerse the average human:

> In order to be **ritually** fit for use, the miḳweh must contain sufficient water to cover entirely the body of a man of average size. The Rabbis estimated that the miḳweh should be 3 cubits long, 1 cubit wide, and 1 cubit deep (= 44,118.375 widths of the thumb; Shulḥan 'Aruk, Yoreh De'ah, 201, 1), containing 40 se'ahs of water …

---

14 *Jewish Virtual Library*, "Jewish Practices & Rituals: Mikveh," https://www.jewishvirtuallibrary.org/jsource/Judaism/mikveh.html.

15 *The Jewish Encyclopedia*, vol. 8, p. 588, s.v. "Mikweh."

16 *Encyclopedia Judaica*, vol. 11, p. 1534, s.v. "Mikveh."

The se'ah is described as a measure holding 144 eggs (Num. R. xviii. 17), *i.e.*, 24 logs (= 24 pints = 3 gallons approximately; see Weights and Measures), so that the miḳweh must contain at least 120 gallons of water.[17]

The disciples were continually meeting in the Temple at Solomon's porch for some time after the Resurrection (Acts 2:46, 3:1, 3:11; 5:12, 19, 20), and this ritual immersion in water (called a baptism, bath, or washing) was required by the authorities before entering the Temple (Acts 21:24–26).

2.7 THESE WATER BAPTISMS ALSO REQUIRED FOR GENTILE PROSELYTES

The Jewish Encyclopedia quotes the Talmud showing that during the time that the Temple existed, **baptism** was also a requirement for a Gentile who would convert to Judaism:

> According to rabbinical teachings, which dominated even during the existence of the Temple (Pes. viii. 8), **Baptism**, next to circumcision and sacrifice, **was an absolutely necessary condition to be fulfilled by a proselyte to Judaism.**[18]

According to rabbinic belief, this water baptism enabled the "unwashed" to be ritually cleansed from idolatry and their uncleanness to become purified, so they could become a part of the commonwealth of Israel:

> The Baptism of the proselyte has for its purpose his cleansing from the impurity of idolatry, and the restoration to the purity of a new-born man. This may be learned from the Talmud (Soṭah 12*b*) in regard to Pharaoh's daughter, whose bathing in the Nile is explained by Simon b. Yoḥai to have been for that purpose. The bathing in the water is to constitute a rebirth,

---

17 *The Jewish Encyclopedia*, vol. 8, p. 588, s.v. "Mikweh."
18 *The Jewish Encyclopedia*, vol. 2, p. 499, s.v. "Baptism."

> wherefore "the ger is like a child just born" (Yeb. 48*b*); and he must bathe "**in the name of God**"—"leshem shamayim"—**that is, assume the yoke of God's kingdom imposed upon him by the one who leads him to Baptism** ("maṭbil"), or else he is not admitted into Judaism (Gerim. vii. 8). For this very reason the Israelites before the acceptance of the Law had, according to Philo on the Decalogue ("De Decalogo," ii., xi.), as well as according to rabbinical tradition, to undergo the rite of baptismal purification (compare **I Cor. x. 2**, "They were baptized unto Moses [the Law] in the clouds and in the sea"). [19]

Notice it quotes 1 Corinthians 10:2, where Paul says they were baptized (washed) "in the clouds and the sea," meaning that they were spiritually (not literally) washed from Egypt. And also notice how "**in the name of God**" in their idiom meant that one assumed the yoke of God's kingdom and all of the teaching that went with that—and that it was not meant as a rigid formula to be spoken verbally, as we will see in the next chapter.

And just as God instructs in Leviticus and Numbers for the ministers to "bathe" before entering the Tabernacle or for ritual cleansing, Jewish sources will often refer to baptism as the "bath," as we see from *The Jewish Encyclopedia* speaking about the proselyte to Judaism under the definition of baptism:

> The expression that **the person baptized** is illuminated (φωτισθείς, Justin, "Apologiæ," i. 65) has the same significance as is implied in telling a proselyte to Judaism, **after his bath**, that he now belongs to Israel, the people beloved of God (Yeb. 47*a*; Gerim i.). [20]

And likewise from the quote we saw earlier from Jewish scholar Moses Maimonides:

---

19 *The Jewish Encyclopedia*, vol. 2, p. 500, s.v. "Baptism."

20 *The Jewish Encyclopedia*, vol. 2, p. 499, s.v. "Baptism."

> Our Sages, as is well known, said, "Even a clean person **may not enter the Sanctuary** for the purpose of performing divine service, **unless he takes previously a bath**."[21]

We see in the New Testament at the Festival of Pentecost that there were proselytes (Acts 2:5–10), and in their idiom, these people would have also needed this ritual baptism into the Jewish faith. Under Moses, the law stated that these proselytes should be treated as one born in the land (Exodus 12:48), assuming they kept God's instructions such as these baptisms/washings and circumcision.

And this gives additional meaning to when Peter, who is coming further into New Covenant truth but is not all of the way there yet, explains in Acts 10 that Gentile believers in the Messiah (whom God just filled with the Holy Spirit) should not be forbidden "the water":

> [NAS] Acts 10:47 "Surely no one can refuse **the water** for these to be baptized who have received the Holy Spirit just as we *did*, can he?"

The term "the water" refers to a specific water—that of ceremonial washing (baptism) that any proselyte would undergo. So Peter, just now in Acts 10, receives the understanding from God that these believing Gentiles were not to be considered unclean (Acts 10:28). And possibly not yet having the revelation that Paul came to on the various water baptisms, Peter orders them to be baptized, for they are now to be accepted into the commonwealth of Israel as proselytes:

> [NAS] Acts 10:48 And he ordered them to be baptized **in the name of** Jesus Christ. Then they asked him to stay on for a few days.

Yet something showed that this baptism was different from the previous Jewish baptisms in that it was to be done with a certain focus;

---

21 Maimonides, *The Guide for the Perplexed*, Part 3, ch. 47, pp. 367–368, http://www.sacred-texts.com/jud/gfp/gfp183.htm.

this baptism was "in the name of" Jesus (meaning it was with that new focus).

※

I have endeavored in this chapter to show a clear history leading up to and including the first century, when various Jewish ceremonial washings in water were synonymous with the use of the word "baptism."

In subsequent chapters, we will explore why the apostle Paul would say that these various ritual washings (**baptisms** in Greek) were imposed only **until** the time that New Covenant came in:

> ᴺᴬᴮ Hebrews 9:10   but only in matters of food and drink and various **ritual washings**: regulations concerning the flesh, **imposed until** the time of the new order.

> ᴳᴺᵀ Hebrews 9:10   μόνον ἐπὶ βρώμασιν καὶ πόμασιν καὶ διαφόροις **βαπτισμοῖς**, δικαιώματα σαρκὸς μέχρι καιροῦ διορθώσεως ἐπικείμενα.

3

The Messiah's Spirit Baptism Supersedes John's Water Baptism

As the Roman Church lost spiritual light and entered the Dark Ages, it was passed down to subsequent generations that its specific kind of water baptism was vitally important. The Messiah's baptism and the Holy Spirit infilling were all but forgotten.

In the New Covenant, believers were supposed to move on to the Messiah's Spirit baptism and be filled with the Holy Spirit, but in the Roman-controlled Church, these truths were derailed and the focus returned to water baptism. The blessings of the Messiah's baptism and the infilling of the Holy Spirit (rest, peace, joy, glory, love, praying in the spirit, and other beneficial aspects) were overlooked by the Roman emphasis on **water** baptism.

3.1 THE MESSIAH WANTED HIS HOLY SPIRIT BAPTISM BROUGHT FORTH, BUT…

John the Baptist understood that the Messiah's baptism would supersede the water baptism that he was called to bring. Notice how John contrasts his water baptism to the Holy Spirit baptism of the Messiah with the use of the word "but":

> NAS Matthew 3:11 "As for me, I baptize you with water for repentance, **but** He who is coming after me is mightier than I, and I am not fit to remove His sandals; **He will baptize you with the Holy Spirit** and fire.

> NAS Mark 1:8 "I baptized you with water; **but** He will baptize you with the Holy Spirit."

John not only contrasts the Messiah's baptism to his own, but he explains how much greater the Messiah is than he:

> ^{NAS} Luke 3:16   John answered and said to them all, "As for me, I baptize you with water; **but** One is coming who **is mightier than I, and I am not fit to untie the thong of His sandals; He will baptize you with the Holy Spirit** and fire.

And we see the same thing in the Gospel of John, contrasting the Messiah's baptism to his own water baptism:

> ^{NAS} John 1:33   "And I did not recognize Him, but He who sent me to baptize in water said to me, 'He upon whom you see the Spirit descending and remaining upon Him, **this is the one who baptizes in the Holy Spirit**.'

And Jesus, after his resurrection but just before he ascends to heaven, shows the disciples this same contrast:

> ^{NAS} Acts 1:5   for John baptized with water, **but** you shall be baptized with the Holy Spirit not many days from now."

The scriptures are clear that God called John to baptize in water (John 1:33), but not one scripture says Jesus was called to baptize *in water*. Now John 3:22–23 does appear at first to show Jesus water baptizing (still in the Old Covenant), but a few verses later, it is clear that Jesus himself is not water baptizing—only his disciples are:

> ^{NAS} John 3:22–23   After these things Jesus and His disciples came into the land of Judea, and there He was spending time with them and baptizing. And John also was baptizing in Aenon near Salim, because there was much water there; and they were coming and were being baptized.

3. The Messiah's Spirit Baptism Supersedes John's Water Baptism 23

^{NAS} John 4:1-2   When therefore the Lord knew that the Pharisees had heard that Jesus was making and baptizing more disciples than John (**although Jesus Himself was not baptizing**, but His disciples were),

Now if God called Jesus to baptize in water, why is Jesus not joining in with his disciples to do God's will like John the Baptist did? The answer is that he was not avoiding God's will, for God never directed him to baptize in water in the first place.

In fact, at various times the Messiah began pointing forward to his New Covenant Spirit baptism. For instance, when the Holy Spirit baptism was poured out upon the believing (but uncircumcised) Gentiles, Peter explains that this contrast in baptisms was something that Jesus had mentioned on numerous occasions:

^{NAS} Acts 11:15   "And as I began to speak, the Holy Spirit fell upon them, just as *He did* upon us at the beginning.

^{NAS} Acts 11:16   "And **I remembered** the word of the Lord, **how He used to say**, 'John baptized with water, **but** you shall be baptized with the Holy Spirit.'

Now Jesus could have said:

"John baptized with water, **and** I will add another baptism to this ritual washing—the Holy Spirit baptism."

However, in this regard, not once did Jesus or John ever say "and." They always used the contrasting "but" because they both knew full well that the Old Covenant water baptism would be replaced by the Messiah's Spirit baptism (the washing/bathing/baptism in God's Spirit). If believers are "washed" by accepting the shed blood of Christ for forgiveness, and thus they have been washed/baptized by the Holy Spirit, do they really still need an additional cleansing of a water baptism at the hands of a priest, pastor, minister, or rabbi?

Paul certainly didn't think so:

> NAS 1 Corinthians 1:14 **I thank God that I baptized none of you** except Crispus and Gaius,

> NAS 1 Corinthians 1:17 For **Christ did not send me to baptize**, but to preach the gospel, not in cleverness of speech, **that the cross of Christ should not be made void**.

Paul understood that the water baptisms were no longer imposed in the New Covenant, and this is why Paul thanked God that he baptized only a few of them, and why he also states here that "Christ did not send me to baptize."

We must consider whether in the New Covenant, the blood of Christ is sufficient to approach God, or if we also need ritual immersion in water (i.e., baptism).

3.2 LIVING WATERS WERE FOR RITUAL WASHINGS UNTIL THE MESSIAH'S BAPTISM

There are, of course, many scriptures on baptism that must be explained, but understanding what water baptism had represented for Israelites for hundreds of years and what the Messiah's promised baptism would be (as contrasted to John's) is a very important foundation for interpreting those New Testament scriptures. These various baptism scriptures will be explained one by one, but for now let's continue with the Messiah's baptism.

His baptism would become available only after his death and resurrection paid the penalty for our sins and washed us in such a way that God's Spirit could freely take up residence within:

> KJV John 16:7 Nevertheless I tell you the truth; It is expedient for you that I go away: **for if I go not away**, the Comforter will not come unto you; but if I depart, I will send him unto you.

Without Jesus paying the price and providing atonement, the Holy Spirit could not be poured out on all flesh (as Joel prophesied in Joel 2:28). This pouring out of the Holy Spirit was the true living water that would be poured out when the Messiah had accomplished his calling:

> ^{NAS} John 7:38-39 "He who believes in Me, as the Scripture said, 'From his innermost being **shall flow rivers of living water.**' " **But this He spoke of the Spirit**, whom those who believed in Him **were to receive; for the Spirit was not yet given**, because Jesus was not yet glorified.

These scriptures show that receiving the Holy Spirit was not to be a one-time event, but that the believer is supposed to have rivers of living water flowing through his innermost being on a continual basis.

In Jewish history, "living water" was associated with ritual purification, referring to a body of moving water such as a river (hence "living" as opposed to a stagnant pond). This was often a requirement for ritual cleansings (baptisms).

The Jewish Encyclopedia shows that waters for baptisms and ritual washings in a *mikveh* or *mikweh* must come from these living waters:

> The water of the miḵweh must come from a natural spring or from a river that has its source in a natural spring (Sifra to Lev. xi. 36). A tank filled by the rain may be used as a miḵweh, although some authorities forbid the use of a pool which is full of water in the rainy season and dried up in the summer (Maimonides, "Yad," Miḵa'ot, iii. 1-3; Yoreh De'ah, 201, 2, Isserles' gloss).[22]

The Hebrew word translated as "running" in the following scripture means "alive, living."

---

22   *The Jewish Encyclopedia*, vol. 8, p. 588, s.v. "Mikweh."

> ᴺᴬˢ Leviticus 15:13 'Now when the man with the discharge becomes cleansed from his discharge, then he shall count off for himself seven days for his cleansing; he shall then wash his clothes and **bathe** his body in **running** water and shall become clean.

During his ministry, Jesus sometimes pointed forward to the true living water, to the "water" (God's Spirit) that would flow out from the believer after Pentecost (John 7:37–39). And below, he promises the *spiritual* living water that the believer would soon receive and give forth—again moving beyond the natural living water:

> ᴺᴬˢ John 4:10 Jesus answered and said to her, "If you knew the gift of God, and who it is who says to you, 'Give Me a drink,' you would have asked Him, and He would have given you **living water**."

> ᴺᴬˢ John 4:11 She said to Him, "Sir, You have nothing to draw with and the well is deep; **where then do You get that living water?**

> ᴺᴬˢ John 4:14 but whoever drinks of the water that I shall give him shall never thirst; but **the water that I shall give him shall become in him a well of water springing up to eternal life**."

Thus, the Messiah brought in the spiritual fountain of living waters that would provide the true washing for all uncleanness:

> ᴷᴶⱽ Zechariah 13:1 In that day there shall be a fountain opened to the house of David and to the inhabitants of Jerusalem for sin and for uncleanness.

3.3 RITUAL WASHINGS IN WATER UNTIL THE RESURRECTION AND NEW ORDER

At the Last Supper (John 13:10), Jesus refers to the natural bathing required for one to enter the Temple (or Tabernacle) and the washing of the feet and hands before ministering, as this was a requirement from God through Moses for ministers in the Tabernacle/Temple:

> ^{NAS} Exodus 30:19 "And Aaron and his sons shall wash their hands and their feet from it;

> ^{NAS} Exodus 30:20 when they enter the tent of meeting, they shall wash with water, that they may not die; or when they approach the altar to minister, by offering up in smoke a fire *sacrifice* to the LORD.

To show the superiority of the cleansing that the Messiah would bring, let's now consider a few New Testament scriptures that bear this out. (Contrary to current popular opinion, the Last Supper was not the Passover because the next day Christ would be crucified, being the exact day that God commanded Moses for the Passover sacrifice. See the many proofs of this in my first book, *The Messianic Feast*).

Jewish history shows that usually two from each group of 10 to 20 people who had gathered for Passover would have the duty of entering the Temple for the slaying of their lamb. This was also the one day in the year where the common Israelite (non-priest) could approach God's altar in the Temple. Usually the leader and one other individual would go from each group, and both were required to be ritually clean for this sacrificial rite, as well as for their partaking of the Passover.

Peter probably believed he would be going, and the conversation with Jesus about washing and being (ritually) clean probably alludes to this (see John 13:10 further below). Jesus was probably also giving a spiritual example of New Covenant truth when he began to wash their feet before the meal (a first-century custom necessitated by walking around hot dusty roads in sandals).

Peter first says, No way Lord, you shall not wash my feet (thinking that the Messiah was too high-ranking for such a thing), but then Jesus responded that if he didn't wash Peter's feet, he would have no part with him (probably symbolically referring to the future New Covenant and how the Lord washes us with the word of God). Then Peter jumps to the other extreme and declares, "Lord, not my feet only, but also my hands and my head" (John 13:5–9). So Jesus answers below in a way that probably refers back to the priests under Moses, when after the ritual bath they needed to wash only their feet and hands at the altar before continuing with certain aspects of their sacrificial ministry:

> NAS John 13:10 Jesus said to him, "He who **has bathed** needs only to wash his feet, but is completely clean; and **you are clean**, but not all *of you*."

The comment about "not all of you" refers to Judas, who in the Lord's eyes was not clean because of the betrayal going on in his heart.

But just after supper, after all this talk about washing their feet and being ritually clean, Jesus says something somewhat shocking to those still under Old Covenant laws and various ritual cleansings. Jesus points further to the coming New Covenant by explaining that it was because of God's word coming through him (and being received by them) that the disciples are clean:

> NAS John 15:3 "You are already **clean because of the word which I have spoken to you.**

The Greek word for clean that Jesus uses in these scriptures is *katharoi*, and it was commonly used for Jewish ceremonial cleansings (Mark 1:44; Luke 2:22; John 3:25). Below, where Jesus/Yeshua turns water into wine, it was the water in the jars used for ritual washings:

> NAB John 2:6 Now there were six stone water jars there for Jewish **ceremonial washings**, each holding twenty to thirty gallons.

The actual word translated as "ceremonial washing" above is again this same Greek word meaning cleansing or purification. In the New Covenant, we are already "bathed" by believing in the Lord and receiving him as our Savior and his shed blood as paying the penalty for our sin. As soon as we believe, we are washed/bathed/baptized (in the name of Jesus) and cleansed from all of our sin. However, as we walk out in this life as a believer, there are times when we fail, our feet get dirty (spiritually speaking), and we need the Lord to wash our feet.

This is what the Apostles came to understand and teach—that in the New Covenant a different way of being cleansed was emerging, and that ritual washings in water were no longer efficacious:

> NIV Hebrews 9:10 They are only a matter of food and drink and various **ceremonial washings—external regulations** applying **until** the time of the new order.

The actual word that Paul used—translated as "ceremonial washings" above—is the Greek word for baptisms in plural form: *baptismos*. Paul is saying that the various baptisms in water no longer apply in the New Covenant (i.e., "new order").

Below, we see Paul using the spiritual application of how New Covenant believers are washed with the word of God:

> NAS Ephesians 5:25 Husbands, love your wives, just as Christ also loved the church and gave Himself up for her;

> NAS Ephesians 5:26 that He might sanctify her, having **cleansed her** by the **washing of water with the word**,

3.4 SPIRITUALLY WASHED WITH THE MESSIAH'S BAPTISM

In the Messiah's New Covenant baptism, the Spirit of God washes and bathes us, and the living water the Messiah gives keeps us clean and forgiven as we walk in his way:

> ʸᴸᵀ Titus 3:5 (**not by works** that *are* in righteousness **that we did** but according to His kindness,) He did save us, through a **bathing of regeneration**, and a **renewing of the Holy Spirit**,

> ᴺᴬˢ 1 John 1:9 If we confess our sins, He is faithful and righteous to **forgive us** our sins and **to cleanse us** from all unrighteousness.

Again, the word for cleanse in the verse above is the same Greek word the Jews often used for ritual cleansings. We no longer need to approach the Temple with sacrifice in hand for forgiveness, but instead we confess our sins to God and receive His cleansing. We no longer need ceremonial cleansings in water because we appropriate the Messiah's shed blood:

> ᴺᴬˢ 1 John 1:7 but if we walk in the light as He Himself is in the light, we have fellowship with one another, and the blood of Jesus His Son **cleanses** us from all sin.

The Messiah's sacrifice brought the fulfillment of the ritual cleansings that were required under the Mosaic covenant:

> ᴺᴬˢ Hebrews 1:3b When He had made **purification** of sins, He sat down at the right hand of the Majesty on high;

The Greek word for purification above is again *katharismon*, and this shows that through the sacrifice Jesus made and by us accepting his shed blood as the penalty for our forgiveness, we become ritually clean before God as we receive this truth and apply it. This makes us fully able to enter God's presence and receive spiritual sustenance.

It is interesting to note that ancient Jewish writings align with this concept and that a "baptism" was required before receiving the Spirit of God. This is from *The Jewish Encyclopedia*:

> To receive the spirit of God, or to be permitted to stand in the presence of God (His Shekinah), man must undergo **Baptism** (Tan., Meẓora', 6, ed. Buber, p. 46), wherefore in the Messianic time God will Himself pour water of purification upon Israel in accordance with Ezek. xxxvi. 25 (Tan., Meẓora', 9–17, 18, ed. Buber, pp. 43, 53).[23]

It is also interesting to note that when Jewish scholars from *The Jewish Encyclopedia* examine the New Testament scriptures, they understand that the Messiah would not baptize in water but with the Holy Spirit:

> The only conception of Baptism at variance with Jewish ideas is displayed in the declaration of John, that the one who would come after him would **not baptize with water**, but with the Holy Ghost (Mark i. 8; John i. 27). Yet a faint resemblance to the notion is displayed in the belief expressed in the Talmud that the Holy Spirit could be drawn upon as water is drawn from a well (based upon Isa. xii. 3; Yer. Suk. v. 1, 55*a* of Joshua b. Levi).[24]

So the scholars in *The Jewish Encyclopedia* see something that almost all Bible commentators since Rome have not seen—that the Messiah would *not* baptize in water.

3.5 BAPTIZE/WASH ALL NATIONS IN WATER?

At what is called the Great Commission, Jesus gives instruction to go out and baptize/wash all nations. However, since Roman times, it seems no one has stopped long enough to determine which baptism he intended—an Old Covenant-style baptism in water (except with a new formula), or the New Covenant baptism that he was to bring in, the Holy Spirit baptism/washing?

---

23 *The Jewish Encyclopedia*, vol. 2, p. 499, s.v. "Baptism."
24 *The Jewish Encyclopedia*, vol. 2, p. 499, s.v. "Baptism."

The best explanation when we consider all of the scriptures and history is that he meant the "washing" that was often pictured when the Jews used this word for baptism (as we saw in chapter 2), but he intended it in the spiritual sense. He uses the common natural-to-spiritual idiom and speaks of his *spiritual* baptism/washing, telling the apostles to make disciples of all the nations by *spiritually* washing/baptizing them "in the name of" (in the authority of) the Father, Son, and Holy Spirit. This is accomplished by teaching them all of the proper doctrine that goes along with understanding the one true God (the Father), the Messiah (the Son), and God's Spirit in action (the Holy Spirit).

> NAS Matthew 28:19 "Go therefore and make disciples of all the nations, **baptizing them in the name of** the Father and the Son and the Holy Spirit,
>
> NAS Matthew 28:20 **teaching them** to observe all that I commanded you; and lo, I am with you always, even to the end of the age."

If the Messiah intended to go back to John's water baptism and not move forward to his spiritual baptism/washing, then why did Paul say "Christ did not send me to baptize," and why did Paul thank God he baptized only a few people in water (1 Corinthians 1:14, 17)? And why did Paul say there was **one baptism** if clearly two were required by God?

> NAS Ephesians 4:5 one Lord, one faith, **one baptism**,

Paul shows that this was the Messiah's *Spirit* baptism:

> NAS 1 Corinthians 12:13 For **by one Spirit** we were **all baptized** into one body, whether Jews or Greeks, whether slaves or free, and we were all made to drink of one Spirit.

Since Jesus was not returning to an Old Covenant water baptism at the Great Commission, there is no mention of water here. He was of course referring to his Spirit baptism—that they should go out teaching all of the nations to receive the true baptizing/washing that is connected to believing in him, and all of the truth that he had taught them (we will examine this verse further in chapter 5):

> ^{NAS} Matthew 28:19 "Go therefore and make disciples of all the nations, **baptizing them in the name of** the Father and the Son and the Holy Spirit,

> ^{NAS} Acts 11:16 "And **I remembered** the word of the Lord, **how He used to say,** 'John baptized with water, **but you shall be baptized with** the Holy Spirit.'

3.6 BAPTISM "IN THE NAME OF" AND HOW ROME MISINTERPRETED IT

As for the Messiah's statement saying, "baptizing them **in the name of** the Father and the Son and the Holy Spirit," this was misunderstood in Rome to be a specific formula of words that a priest should recite over each water baptism recipient (i.e., along the lines of "I now baptize you in the name of the Father, and of the Son, and of the Holy Spirit").

Here is this Roman Catholic formula, according to *The Catholic Encyclopedia*:

> Baptism: Form
>
> The **requisite and sole valid form of baptism** is: "I baptize thee (or This person is baptized) **in the name of** the Father and of the Son and of the Holy Ghost." This was the form given by Christ to His Disciples in the twenty-eighth chapter of St. Matthew's Gospel, as far, at least, as there is question of the invocation of the separate Persons of the Trinity and the expression of the nature of the action performed. [25]

---

25   Herbermann et al, *The Catholic Encyclopedia*, vol. 2, p. 262, s.v. "Baptism."

Many Protestants disagreed with this formula. Although they agreed with Rome that there should be a formula of some kind, they thought it should be, "I now baptize you in the name of Jesus."

They went with this set of words based on how they interpreted certain scriptures that seemed to say that was the correct formula used by the apostles (Acts 2:38, 8:16, 10:48, 19:5). They did not believe that the words of Jesus in Matthew 28:19 meant that the long version was the correct formula.

However, a formula of words was never used in the Jewish ceremonial cleansings (baptisms). There is no record that John the Baptist ever said, "I now baptize you in the name of John" before each water baptism. Nor did the Jews recite a name before each baptism they were involved with, saying, "I now baptize you in the name of Rabbi Gamaliel" or "I now baptize this cup in the name of Rabbi Akiva." Nor did Naaman baptize himself "in the name of Elisha" in what we saw was effectively the first Jewish baptism. Baptizing "in the name of" was simply the Jewish idiom of referring to whose baptism and whose doctrine or authority in which something was done and what the focus of that baptizing/washing was.

Thus, the words of Jesus in that portion of scripture called the Great Commission were later misunderstood in Rome to mean a prescribed formula for water baptism, and this has been handed down in various ways ever since.

As a side note, some researchers dispute the portion of scripture containing the Roman Catholic formula for Matthew 28:19 ("in the name of the Father, and the Son, and the Holy Spirit"), arguing that it was a later addition to that verse (possibly around the time of the Council of Nicea).

They quote alternate endings for that scripture based on early writings by Greek historian Eusebius (ca. AD 260 to ca. 340) that exclude the word "baptizing" and end with "make disciples of all nations in my name." Interestingly, the only other scripture where Jesus mentions baptism such that it could possibly refer to water is in another contested scripture. Many scholars believe that the ending of Mark 16:9–20 may not be original due to the manuscript evidence.[26] For the purpose of this study, I explain both scriptures, assuming that they were original scripture. It is of note, however, that the parallel passage in Luke to these two contested baptism scriptures does not actually include the word "baptism":

> [NAS] Luke 24:47   and that repentance for forgiveness of sins should be proclaimed **in His name** to all the nations, beginning from Jerusalem.

This "repentance for forgiveness of sins" was proclaimed "in His name," and this was the true spiritual baptism/washing that the Messiah brought in for all who believe, and this is what Paul and the other apostles would come to understand.

3.7   WHAT EXACTLY DID "IN THE NAME OF" MEAN IN THE JEWISH IDIOM?

When Jesus told the disciples in the scriptures covered above to go out baptizing/washing the nations "in the name of…," he was not referring to a new formula for water baptism. Thus, the following verse did not mean that with every step or every breath one takes, one must say "in the name of" prior to taking it:

> [NAS] Colossians 3:17   And **whatever you do in word or deed**, *do* all **in the name of** the Lord Jesus, giving thanks through Him to God the Father.

---

26 Some manuscripts are considered to be more important than others for various reasons (the age of the manuscript, etc.). In the case of Mark 16, the more esteemed manuscripts end at verse 8. Other scholars think that the last page of this manuscript may have been physically removed from or not retained in certain copies, and that is why verses 9–20 of Mark 16 are omitted. They argue that the gospel would not end at the death of Jesus without even a mention of his appearance to the disciples after his resurrection, which other manuscripts include. It was the version with the longer ending that was originally recognized as canonical. So, there is scholarly debate as well as manuscript evidence that go into determining the original reading for those rare scriptures that have variants that could affect doctrine.

Again, this was not a phrase to be recited over every single word a person spoke or every deed done. Rather, it was a Jewish manner of speaking that often pointed out the authority or focus in which something was done:

> ᴺᴬˢ John 14:26 "But the Helper, the Holy Spirit, whom the Father will send **in My name**, He will teach you all things, and bring to your remembrance all that I said to you.

> ᴺᴬˢ Acts 4:18 And when they had summoned them, they commanded them not to speak or teach at all **in the name of Jesus**.

> ᴷᴶⱽ Acts 3:6 Then Peter said, Silver and gold have I none; but such as I have give I thee: **In the name of** Jesus Christ of Nazareth rise up and walk.

We see this "in the name of" repeatedly in earlier Jewish history as well:

> ᴷᴶⱽ Deuteronomy 18:5 For the LORD thy God hath chosen him out of all thy tribes, to stand to minister **in the name of** the LORD,[27] him and his sons for ever.

And a prophet speaking for the false gods would speak **in the name of** them:

> ᴷᴶⱽ Deuteronomy 18:20 But the prophet, which shall presume to speak a word in my name, which I have not commanded him to speak, or that shall speak **in the name of** other gods, even that prophet shall die.

> ᴺᴬˢ Micah 4:5 Though all the peoples walk Each **in the name of** his god, As for us, we will walk **In the name of** the LORD our God forever and ever.

---

27 The Hebrew here reads "in the name of YHWH" (i.e., it is "Yahweh" whenever LORD is in all capital letters).

David was not reciting a formula when he came out to face Goliath:

> ^{KJV} 1 Samuel 17:45   Then said David to the Philistine, Thou comest to me with a sword, and with a spear, and with a shield: but I come to thee **in the name of** the LORD of hosts, the God of the armies of Israel, whom thou hast defied.

It was not a formula that David's men used when they brought David's word to Nabal:

> ^{KJV} 1 Samuel 25:9   And when David's young men came, they spake to Nabal according to all those words **in the name of** David, and ceased.

Then, in New Testament times, certain nonbeliever exorcists started using the name of Jesus as part of their new technique:

> ^{DBY} Acts 19:13   And certain of the Jewish exorcists also, who went about, took in hand to call upon those who had wicked spirits the name of the Lord Jesus, saying, **I adjure you by Jesus**, whom Paul preaches.

But they quickly discovered that it was not to be used as a magical word. One had to actually be a disciple—an extension of the authority of Jesus—to go forth with his power:

> ^{NAS} Acts 19:15–16   And the evil spirit answered and said to them, "I recognize Jesus, and I know about Paul, but who are you?" And the man, in whom was the evil spirit, leaped on them and subdued all of them and overpowered them, so that they fled out of that house naked and wounded.

Again, the following verse does not mean that we are to recite a formula over each new believer, declaring, "you are now justified **in the name of Jesus**":

> ^{NAS} 1 Corinthians 6:11   And such were some of you; but you were washed, but you were sanctified, but you were justified **in the name of** the Lord Jesus Christ, and in the Spirit of our God.

As we saw earlier in chapter 2, "in the name of" in the early Jewish idiom did not refer to a set of words that must be recited out loud. We saw this in the *Jewish Encyclopedia*'s definition of baptism, which quoted the writers of the Talmud discussing "in the name of God":

> The Baptism of the proselyte has for its purpose his cleansing from the impurity of idolatry, and the restoration to the purity of a new-born man. This may be learned from the Talmud (Soṭah 12*b*) in regard to Pharaoh's daughter, whose bathing in the Nile is explained by Simon b. Yoḥai to have been for that purpose. The bathing in the water is to constitute a rebirth, wherefore "the ger is like a child just born" (Yeb. 48*b*); and he must bathe **"in the name of God"**—"leshem shamayim"— **that is, assume the yoke of God's kingdom imposed upon him by the one who leads him to Baptism** ("maṭbil"), or else he is not admitted into Judaism (Gerim. vii. 8). [28]

To these early Jews, bathe (baptize) "in the name of God" was not a phrase to be recited at baptism but rather an assumption of the spiritual yoke, authority, and teaching of the one in whose name one was baptized. And once again, it was in Rome where this idiom was misunderstood to be a set formula of words spoken aloud during a Roman Catholic–approved water baptism.

There were, of course, times when the disciples used the name of Jesus in various statements concerning baptism (Acts 2:38; 10:48; 19:5), but among these early Jews it was not a ritualistic formula to be spoken before each event as came about later in Rome. For instance, the following verse did not mean that every time the apostles spoke or taught, they invoked a formula of "I now speak to you in the name of Jesus":

---

28   *The Jewish Encyclopedia*, vol. 2, p. 500, s.v. "Baptism."

> NAS Acts 5:40 And they took his advice; and after calling the apostles in, they flogged them and ordered them to **speak no more in the name of Jesus,** and *then* released them.

As with the examples covered earlier, it meant that they were teaching the truths they had received concerning Jesus, speaking and doing miracles with a focus on him.

So in the book of Acts, when the scripture speaks of the group of believers who have not yet received the Holy Spirit infilling (because it says they had only been **baptized/washed "in the name of"** Jesus), it did not necessarily mean a formula was invoked over them. It may not even refer to *water* baptism but to the "washing" that comes with believing:

> NAS Acts 8:16 For He had not yet fallen upon any of them; they had simply been baptized **in the name** of the Lord Jesus.

Once these believers were "washed" in the name of Jesus by believing in the Messiah and all that went with that belief, they were then prepared to receive the Holy Spirit within:

> NAS Acts 8:17 Then they *began* laying their hands on them, and they were receiving the Holy Spirit.

You can clearly see the two steps to the Holy Spirit infilling above. We are first baptized/washed as soon as we believe in the Messiah and accept his sacrifice for our cleansing from sin, and then we are thus prepared to be filled with the Holy Spirit as we receive this gift of God, such as the following examples in the book of Acts (Acts 2:3–4; 8:15–17; 19:5–6).

This is true for several scriptures in the book of Acts, such as when Paul comes across a group of disciples in Ephesus and he asks them if they received the Holy Spirit **when** they believed:

> NAS Acts 19:2a and he said to them, "Did you receive the Holy Spirit when you believed?"

And when they say they have not, then Paul prays for them and they are filled with the Spirit and speak in tongues (Acts 19:6).

The Messiah's Holy Spirit baptism takes place when we believe—that is, when we are washed (baptized) and cleansed, as Peter taught:

> ^NIV Acts 10:43 All the prophets testify about him that everyone who believes in him receives forgiveness of sins **through his name**."

Remember, all of the scriptures at the beginning of this chapter contrast John's water baptism with the moving forward into the Messiah's Spirit baptism that would take place during the promised New Covenant:

> ^NAS Mark 1:8 "I baptized you with water; **but** He will baptize you with the Holy Spirit."

When all of these facts are taken together, it becomes clear that the baptism Jesus spoke of at the Great Commission was the promised baptism he would bring; he was not called by God to bring a water baptism like John was.

4

How the Natural-to-Spiritual Idiom among the Jews Explains Many Baptism Scriptures

"The spiritual did not come first, but the natural, and after that the spiritual."

— ^{NIV} 1 Corinthians 15:46 —

My previous book, *The Messianic Feast: Moving Beyond the Ritual*, includes a 19-page chapter filled with examples of how the Jewish natural-to-spiritual idiom was used in the first century and also in the scriptures. We won't go into that degree of depth here but will provide a few examples to prepare the reader to look at certain baptism scriptures in the way they were *meant*, not simply by what they say.

In other words, early Jewish Messianic followers often used many terms figuratively, whereby they did not actually *mean* the natural or literal object, but the spiritual truth or aspect behind it. To properly interpret many scriptures on baptism, this natural-to-spiritual idiom must be understood.

No better example of this natural-to-spiritual idiom is seen than with the Jewish washings and baptisms (including John's). They were *naturally* washed and baptized with water under the Old Covenant and then *spiritually* washed and baptized with God's Spirit in the New Covenant.

And John's quote that contrasts his water baptism to the Messiah's Holy Spirit baptism is a perfect natural-to-spiritual example. After all, you cannot literally baptize (wash, immerse, dip) in the Spirit because it is a spiritual phenomenon. The scripture uses a natural word for something that is a spiritual occurrence:

> NAS Mark 1:8 "I baptized you with water; but He will baptize you with the Holy Spirit."

And although the scriptures show Jesus pouring this out from heaven onto the believers (Acts 2:32, 33), this, of course, is not what literally happens. He does not actually have a pitcher filled with the Holy Spirit that he pours out onto people from heaven. Again, it is a natural picture to help explain a spiritual occurrence.

When Peter preached to the uncircumcised Gentiles and the Holy Spirit was poured out onto them, Peter remembers the natural-to-spiritual baptism statements that the Lord had been saying to them:

> NAS Acts 11:16 "And I remembered the word of the Lord, **how He used to say**, 'John baptized with water, but you shall be baptized with the Holy Spirit.'

The next two sections will cover several more examples of this first-century Jewish idiom, where they say the *natural* word but mean the *spiritual* truth behind it.

4.1   THEY WERE NOW IN THE PROMISED NEW COVENANT

As the Jewish believers became more familiar with being in the New Covenant, they saw that almost everything from the Old Covenant now pointed forward to spiritual truth. Paul writes to the Hebrews, saying, "we have an altar," but that is not what he meant literally:

> NAS Hebrews 13:10 We have an altar, from which those who serve the tabernacle have no right to eat.

Paul is contrasting the spiritual altar that believers have with the sacrificial one in the Tabernacle (and Temple) from which the priests could partake, saying that those who serve the Old Covenant have no right to feed on the spiritual food in the New Covenant. One must first be washed by believing in the Messiah before they can share from this spiritual altar. If people go on an archeological dig searching for the lost altar of Paul, they will not find it because he was using a natural-to-spiritual idiom common in his time, not speaking of a literal altar.

Acts 10 and 11 mark a major event in this new understanding, when God fills the uncircumcised Gentiles with the Holy Spirit right after they hear Peter preaching and believe. This was very shocking to Jewish believers, and at first they were upset that Peter had gone in to eat with uncircumcised Gentiles (Acts 11:13).

Peter then goes on to explain to them the vision that God gave him—to not call common what He had cleansed—and how the Holy Spirit fell on them just as it had on the Jews at Pentecost. Peter says, who am I to stand in the way of what God was doing? And to their credit, they realized that since God has accepted these Gentiles, then so should they:

> NAS Acts 11:17–18 "If God therefore gave to them the same gift as *He gave* to us also after believing in the Lord Jesus Christ, who was I that I could stand in God's way?" And when they heard this, they quieted down, and glorified God, saying, "Well then, God has granted to the Gentiles also the repentance *that leads* to life."

Peter even directed these uncircumcised Gentiles to then be baptized/washed, which was a requirement for any Gentile proselyte to become accepted in Israel (see Acts 10:48, with the quote from *The Jewish Encyclopedia* in chapter 2). God would never have poured out His Holy Spirit on uncircumcised Gentiles in the Old Covenant, for circumcision was a requirement of the law.

Events like this caused Paul and the others to understand that they were now under the New Covenant that had long been promised by the Jewish prophets:

> NAS Jeremiah 31:31–32 "Behold, days are coming," declares the LORD, "when I will make **a new covenant** with the house of Israel and with the house of Judah, **not like the covenant which I made with their fathers** in the day I took

them by the hand to bring them out of the land of Egypt, My covenant which they broke, although I was a husband to them," declares the LORD.

^{NAS} Hebrews 8:6 But now He has obtained a more excellent ministry, by as much as He is also the mediator of **a better covenant**, which **has been enacted** on better promises.

4.2 SPIRITUAL TRUTH AND PARABLES

The scripture says that Jesus/Yeshua very often spoke in parables:

^{NAS} Mark 4:33–34 ³³ And with many such parables He was speaking the word to them as they were able to hear it; ³⁴ and He did not speak to them without a parable; but He was explaining everything privately to His own disciples.

He also often used the natural-to-spiritual idiom when speaking, where he spoke natural/literal words but meant them in a spiritual sense. After making many controversial statements in John, chapter 6, he explains that he did not mean them literally but rather was speaking spiritual truth:

^{NIV} John 6:63 The Spirit gives life; the flesh counts for nothing. **The words I have spoken to you are spirit and they are life.**

There are manifold examples of this, such as where the disciples were concerned that he had not been eating enough food, and he responds:

^{NAS} John 4:32 But He said to them, "I have food to eat that you do not know about."

He of course was not referring to natural but spiritual food. The scriptures contain many statements that various Bible commentators have misunderstood because they interpreted them as literal or natural when

4. Natural-to-Spiritual Idiom Explains Many Baptism Scriptures 45

they were actually meant in a spiritual sense. Disciples in the Messiah's day also did this, thinking that he meant natural food in the verse above:

> ^{NAS} John 4:33   The disciples therefore were saying to one another, "No one brought Him *anything* to eat, did he?"

But if we stay open to truth, the Lord can change our perspective to see things the way he intended them:

> ^{NAS} John 4:34   Jesus said to them, "My food is to do the will of Him who sent Me, and to accomplish His work.

Jesus very often spoke in this manner, such as when he compares himself to manna, the natural food that sustained them in the wilderness (called "bread of heaven" in Psalm 105:40). The Messiah shows that he is the *spiritual* food that sustains us by saying that he is the true bread:

> ^{NAS} John 6:32   Jesus therefore said to them, "Truly, truly, I say to you, it is not Moses who has given you the bread out of heaven, but it is My Father who gives you the **true bread** out of heaven.

Below he speaks of bread, hungering, thirsting, and eating, but none of these are meant naturally—rather, he intended spiritual truth:

> ^{NAS} John 6:35   Jesus said to them, "I am the bread of life; he who comes to Me shall **not hunger**, and he who believes in Me shall **never thirst**.

> ^{NAS} John 6:51   "I am the living bread that came down out of heaven; if anyone eats of this bread, he shall live forever;

Many commentators have misunderstood Jesus in the scriptures below where he said he came down from heaven, thinking he meant this literally and had previously lived in heaven:

> ^{NAS} John 6:38 "For **I have come down from heaven**, not to do My own will, but the will of Him who sent Me.
>
> ^{NAS} John 6:41 The Jews therefore were grumbling about Him, because He said, "**I am the bread that came down out of heaven**."

But the Messiah was only comparing himself to the manna, called the bread of heaven. He was using the natural-to-spiritual idiom, saying he was the *spiritual* bread from God that the *natural* manna pointed to.

Although this idiom was especially common among New Covenant believers, it was a long-standing idiom that Jews had always used, such as when the prophet Jeremiah said he "ate" the words of God:

> ^{NAS} Jeremiah 15:16a Thy words were found and I ate them, And Thy words became for me a joy and the delight of my heart;

4.3 OLD COVENANT EVENTS, SACRIFICES, AND SERVICES ALL POINT FORWARD

The final aspect of this idiom that I will focus on is how all of the things in the Old Covenant symbolized, pointed forward, and had spiritual counterparts in the New Covenant, as Paul wrote to the Hebrews:

> ^{NAS} Hebrews 9:24 For Christ did not enter a holy place made with hands, a *mere* copy of the true one, but into heaven itself, now to appear in the presence of God for us;

He understood that things in the Law pointed forward to spiritual truth in the New Covenant:

> ^{NAS} Hebrews 10:1 For the Law, since it has *only* **a shadow of the good things to come** *and* not the very form of things, can never by the same sacrifices year by year, which they offer continually, make perfect those who draw near.

In the Old Covenant, there was a natural altar that required priests to wash before approaching and ministering at it. Just as this altar pointed forward to spiritual truth, so did the required washings—natural washings took place in the Old Covenant and spiritual washings in the New Covenant:

> NAS Exodus 30:20   when they enter the tent of meeting, they shall **wash with water**, that they may not die; or when they approach the altar to minister, by offering up in smoke a fire *sacrifice* to the LORD.

> NAS Ephesians 5:25–26   Husbands, love your wives, just as Christ also loved the church and gave Himself up for her; that He might sanctify her, having cleansed her by the **washing** of water **with the word**,

> NIV Titus 3:5   he saved us, not because of righteous things we had done, but because of his mercy. He saved us through the **washing** of rebirth and renewal **by the Holy Spirit**,

> NAS 1 Corinthians 6:11   And such were some of you; **but you were washed**, but you were sanctified, but you were justified **in the name of** the Lord Jesus Christ, and **in the Spirit of our God**.

In the New Covenant, we are not washed by the ritual washings in water but baptized/washed by God's Spirit:

> KJV 1 Corinthians 12:13   For **by one Spirit** are we all **baptized** into one body, whether *we be* Jews or Gentiles, whether *we be* bond or free; and have been all made to drink into one Spirit.

> NAS 1 Corinthians 6:11   And such were some of you; but **you were washed**, but you were sanctified, but you were justified

> **in the name of** the Lord Jesus Christ, and **in the Spirit of our God**.
>
> ᴺᴬˢ Hebrews 10:22   let us draw near with a sincere heart in full assurance of faith, having **our hearts sprinkled** *clean* from an evil conscience and **our bodies washed with pure water**.

In the Old Covenant, the blood of the sacrifice was *naturally* applied on the altar, whereas in the New Covenant we *spiritually* apply the blood:

> ᴺᴬˢ Hebrews 9:22   And according to the Law, *one may* almost *say*, all things are cleansed with blood, and without shedding of blood there is no forgiveness.
>
> ᴺᴬˢ 1 John 1:7   but if we walk in the light as He Himself is in the light, we have fellowship with one another, and the blood of Jesus His Son cleanses us from all sin.

In the Old Covenant, Moses sprinkled the blood of the sacrifice on the people to sanctify them and inaugurate the Covenant, but in the New Covenant we do this spiritually:

> ᴺᴬˢ Exodus 24:8   So **Moses took the blood and sprinkled** *it* **on the people**, and said, "Behold **the blood of the covenant**, which the LORD has made with you in accordance with all these words."
>
> ᴺᴬˢ 1 Peter 1:2   according to the foreknowledge of God the Father, by the sanctifying work of the Spirit, that **you may obey Jesus Christ and be sprinkled with His blood**: May grace and peace be yours in fullest measure.

And of course, there was the natural Passover lamb and the true spiritual Passover lamb:

> ^{NAS} 1 Corinthians 5:7   Clean out the old leaven, that you may be a new lump, just as you are *in fact* unleavened. For Christ our Passover also has been sacrificed.

Below, Paul did not mean we literally drink God's Spirit—he of course meant we spiritually drink it:

> ^{NAS} 1 Corinthians 12:13   For by one Spirit we were all baptized into one body, whether Jews or Greeks, whether slaves or free, **and we were all made to drink of one Spirit.**

Jesus was not speaking of literal water baptism below but was using the term in a spiritual sense—in this case, of being immersed into a fiery trial:

> ^{NAS} Luke 12:50   "But I have **a baptism** to undergo, and how distressed I am until it is accomplished!

Paul spoke of circumcision here but not a natural one—only of being *spiritually* circumcised:

> ^{NAS} Colossians 2:11   and in Him **you were also circumcised** with a circumcision made **without hands,** in the removal of the body of the flesh by the circumcision of Christ;

Just as circumcision is "by the spirit" as this verse below says, so is water baptism now also fulfilled "by the spirit" (meaning the Messiah's Spirit baptism):

> ^{NAS} Romans 2:29   But he is a Jew who is one inwardly; and circumcision is that which is of the heart, **by the Spirit**, not by the letter; and his praise is not from men, but from God.

> ^{NAS} John 1:33   "And I did not recognize Him, but He who **sent me to baptize in water** said to me, 'He upon whom you

see the Spirit descending and remaining upon Him, **this is the one who baptizes in the Holy Spirit.**'

In the New Covenant, it's not those who are led by water (baptism) who are the sons of God, but those led by God's Spirit, having received the Messiah's Spirit baptism:

> ᴺᴬˢ Romans 8:14   For all who are being led by the Spirit of God, these are sons of God.

Conclusion: Because of their clear natural-to-spiritual idiom when these Jewish disciples speak of being "baptized" or "washed," we want to be careful to not leap to the assumption that they are always referring to a natural water baptism or being literally washed in water, because often they mean these as they did with so many Old Covenant terms—where they are used spiritually in the light of New Covenant fulfillment. Whether undergoing circumcision (without hands), drinking (of God's Spirit), being sprinkled with Christ's blood, finding the lost altar of Paul, or being baptized/washed, we need to always consider the context and not assume it is natural when it may be intended as spiritual truth.

5

Spiritually Washed, Not Baptized in Water

As we've seen before, believers living in Old Covenant times stayed in proper communion with God through the shed blood of sacrifices and the various ritual washings in water that were often required. In the New Covenant, they understood that they were *spiritually* washed by believing that the Messiah paid the penalty for sin, and they were cleansed by appropriating his sacrifice and his shed blood.

In this chapter, we will focus on how the early Jewish teachers (especially Paul), knowing they were then in the promised New Covenant, were not focusing on water baptism but the spiritual washing the Messiah provides. We will also discover how key scriptures have been misunderstood because of the Roman Church's narrow focus on water baptism and their overlooking of Jewish idioms.

5.1 NEW COVENANT: WERE THEY BAPTIZED/WASHED IN WATER, OR SPIRITUALLY WASHED/BAPTIZED?

> NAS 1 Corinthians 6:11 And such were some of you; but **you were washed**, but you were sanctified, but you were justified in the name of the Lord Jesus Christ, and in the Spirit of our God.

> NAS Hebrews 10:22 let us draw near with a sincere heart in full assurance of faith, having our hearts sprinkled *clean* from an evil conscience and **our bodies washed** with pure water.

As seen in 1 Corinthians, Paul thanked God that he baptized only a few people because Christ did not send him to baptize/wash. Therefore, he is not here teaching that they should be "washed" through water baptism. We know this because as we have seen in the previous chapter of Hebrews, Paul said that the various ritual "washings" were no longer imposed when the New Covenant came:

> ^{NAB} Hebrews 9:9-10   This is a symbol of the present time, in which gifts and sacrifices are offered that cannot perfect the worshiper in conscience but only in matters of food and drink and **various ritual washings**: regulations concerning the flesh, **imposed until** the time of the new order.

As was pointed out previously, the actual word that Paul used above, translated as "ritual washings," was the Greek word for **baptisms** (*baptismos*). He understood that the baptisms in water that were required under the Old Covenant for cleansing and sanctification were no longer imposed in the New Covenant, which had been enacted by the Messiah. They were now sanctified and cleansed by what Christ had accomplished, by his shed blood:

> ^{NAS} Hebrews 10:10   By this will we have been **sanctified** through the offering of the body of Jesus Christ once for all.

> ^{NAS} Hebrews 8:6   But now He has obtained a more excellent ministry, by as much as He is also the mediator of **a better covenant**, which **has been enacted** on **better** promises.

One of these "better promises" was the promise of the Father, which was the gift of the Holy Spirit that would be poured out in the promised New Covenant. This outpouring took place fifty days after the Resurrection, on the day of Pentecost:

> ^{NAS} Luke 24:49   "And behold, I am sending forth the **promise of My Father** upon you; but you are to stay in the city until you are clothed with power from on high."

> ^{NAS} Acts 2:4   And they were all **filled with the Holy Spirit** and began to speak with other tongues, as the Spirit was giving them utterance.

> ^{NAS} Acts 2:33 "Therefore having been exalted to the right hand of God, and having received **from the Father the promise of the Holy Spirit**, He has poured forth this which you both see and hear.

Thus, we are not to be naturally washed in water, but spiritually washed and cleansed by God's Spirit, since Christ's shed blood provides that atonement:

> ^{KJV} Revelation 7:14 And I said unto him, Sir, thou knowest. And he said to me, These are they which came out of great tribulation, and have **washed** their robes, and made them white **in the blood of the Lamb**.

> ^{NAS} 1 John 1:7 but if we walk in the light as He Himself is in the light, we have fellowship with one another, and **the blood** of Jesus His Son **cleanses us** from all sin.

> ^{NAS} 1 Corinthians 12:13 For **by one Spirit** we were **all baptized** into one body, whether Jews or Greeks, whether slaves or free, and we were all made to drink of one Spirit.

5.2 BAPTIZE/WASH IN THE NATURAL-TO-SPIRITUAL IDIOM

Chapter 4 examined this common idiom of the Jews and how they used it in multiple ways, and here we will see how this natural-to-spiritual usage was used with their word for baptism. The Messiah set the stage for understanding baptism from a spiritual perspective. As Peter explains, the Lord **used to tell them** that they would be baptized not in water but with the Holy Spirit:

> ^{NAS} Acts 11:16 "And I remembered the word of the Lord, how He used to say, 'John baptized with water, **but you** shall be **baptized with the Holy Spirit**.'

Of course, this Spirit baptism of which the Messiah spoke was an entirely different kind of baptism. The baptisms that the Jews had previously been familiar with were all various water baptisms (also called washing, bathing, etc.). And as we saw before, when these English translations are translated correctly, these baptisms existed long before Jesus and John the Baptist:

> ᴺᴬˢ Luke 11:37 Now when He had spoken, a Pharisee asked Him to have lunch with him; and He went in, and reclined *at the table.*

> ᴺᴬˢ Luke 11:38 And when the Pharisee saw it, he was surprised that He had not first **ceremonially washed** before the meal.

> ᴳᴺᵀ Luke 11:38 ὁ δὲ Φαρισαῖος ἰδὼν ἐθαύμασεν ὅτι οὐ πρῶτον **ἐβαπτίσθη** πρὸ τοῦ ἀρίστου.

I have boldfaced the Greek word for baptism above, and Young's Literal Translation (which is often more accurate to the original Greek than various other translations) makes it clear that the actual Greek word used by Luke in this verse was "baptism":

> ʸᴸᵀ Luke 11:38 and the Pharisee having seen, did wonder that he did not first **baptize himself** before the dinner.

This certainly does not align with the Roman version of baptism that has been handed down to us, where another baptizes you and speaks out a certain formula. As we saw earlier, these Jewish baptisms or washings sometimes involved immersing the whole body in the *mikveh* before entering the Temple or immersing the hands for ritual cleansing, such as before eating the Showbread in the Temple.

Below is another set of scriptures where the Jewish "baptism" does not align with the Roman Catholic-style baptism the Protestants inherited:

> ᴷᴶⱽ Mark 7:2-4   And when they saw some of his disciples eat bread with defiled, that is to say, with unwashen, hands, they found fault. For the Pharisees, and all the Jews, except they wash *their* hands oft, eat not, holding the tradition of the elders. And *when they come* from the market, except they **wash**, they eat not. And many other things there be, which they have received to hold, *as* the **washing** of cups, and pots, brasen vessels, and of tables.

Again, the words I have boldfaced ("wash," "washing") are the Greek words for baptize and baptisms, as Young's Literal again brings out:

> ʸᴸᵀ Mark 7:3-4   for the Pharisees, and all the Jews, if they do not **wash the hands to the wrist**, do not eat, holding the tradition of the elders, and, *coming* from the market-place, if they do not **baptize themselves**, they do not eat; and many other things there are that they received to hold, **baptisms** of cups, and pots, and brazen vessels, and couches.

These verses and the earlier history we covered reveal that in the Jewish idiom, the words "wash" and "baptize" were almost interchangeable. So as we come to the New Testament with the often-used idiom of natural to spiritual (where they use a natural or literal term but intend the spiritual truth behind it), we must not leap to an assumption that every time we see the word "baptized" or "washed," it refers to a *water* baptism. Tradition from Rome has essentially taught us to put on water baptism glasses, so that we automatically picture water every time we see the word "baptism." In the Jewish Messianic idiom, it could have easily meant *spiritually* washed instead.

This is especially true because of the following points:

1. When we consider a particular scripture on baptism, are we sure that it is going backward to the same **water** baptism John brought forth, except in the name of Jesus? Or is it referring to the Messiah's Spirit baptism? The ev-

idence shows that many or even most are talking about the washing (baptism) that comes when one believes in Jesus (the same washing the Jews were accustomed to but in a spiritual sense by accepting the forgiveness Messiah provided).

2. It may seem surprising, but not a single scripture exists where Jesus ever specifically said anyone should water baptize believers. He does say that John's Old Covenant baptism was from God (and living in the Old Covenant, he himself was baptized by John). But he always says that New Covenant believers would be baptized in the Holy Spirit, and not once does he specify that they should also receive *water* baptism. There are several times where he mentions baptism generically (some are clearly figurative, such as Mark 10:38), but in other scriptures, commentators from the time of Rome have assumed he meant it as a water rite. In every instance, it makes much more sense that he was speaking of the Spirit baptism (washing) that he, God, John the Baptist, and Peter all said the Messiah would bring (John 1:33; Acts 1:5; 11:16).

3. And why do Jesus and John contrast the coming baptism that Jesus would bring by saying "but" every time when they refer to the Messiah's coming baptism? Shouldn't they instead say "and"? (Example: "I baptize with water, **and** he will add another baptism to my water baptism, his will be in the Holy Spirit," instead of "I baptized you with water; **but** He will baptize you with the Holy Spirit" (Mark 1:8).

4. If water baptism was really to continue alongside the Messiah's Spirit baptism in the New Covenant, why does Paul say "Christ did not send me to baptize?" (1 Corinthians 1:17).

5. And why does Paul say there is one baptism (Ephesians 4:5) if there are clearly still two baptisms (water baptism and the Messiah's Spirit baptism)?

6. And why does Paul state that the various Old Covenant baptisms have ceased (translated as "washings" by most English versions, but the Greek word is again **baptisms**):

   ^{NAB} Hebrews 9:9 This is a symbol of the present time, in which gifts and sacrifices are offered that cannot perfect the worshiper in conscience

   ^{NAB} Hebrews 9:10 but only in matters of food and drink and various **ritual washings**: regulations concerning the flesh, **imposed until** the time of the new order.

   Again, the actual Greek word here for ritual washings is **baptisms**, as Young's Literal Translation shows:

   ^{YLT} Hebrews 9:10 only in victuals, and drinks, and different **baptisms**, and fleshly ordinances—till the time of reformation imposed upon *them*.

7. And worse yet, why would Paul actually thank God that he baptized only a few people (1 Corinthians 1:14–17) if Jesus meant **water** baptism when he commanded the apostles to baptize the nations at the Great Commission? (More on this in the next section.)

5.3 VIEWING CERTAIN SCRIPTURES THROUGH THE PROPER LENS

We always want to consider the scriptures from the point of view and known idioms of the people who wrote them. We have seen among various historical Jewish writers that the words "baptism" and "washing" were used somewhat interchangeably. We have also seen that they had an existing idiom that was a very common way of saying a natural thing but actually meaning spiritual fulfillment.

Indeed, with all of these points in mind, let's take another look at certain scriptures and see if it helps to see them in a new light that is different from the Roman Catholic (and later Protestant) picture of baptism that has been handed down. Probably the most important verse incorrectly believed to be the Messiah's instruction to go out *water* baptizing the nations is called the "Great Commission"; therefore, we will consider it first:

> NAS Matthew 28:19–20 "Go therefore and make disciples of all the nations, **baptizing** them **in the name of** the Father and the Son and the Holy Spirit, **teaching them to observe all** that I commanded you; and lo, I am with you always, even to the end of the age."

First of all, notice that this does not say to go forth *water* baptizing them. So, this could refer either to a ritual immersion in water (the baptisms that Paul said were no longer imposed) or to the Messiah's Spirit baptism. The latter would mean to go wash them spiritually by bringing the teaching relating to "the father and the Son and the Holy Spirit." The Bible translators also understood that this Greek word for baptize meant wash/washing in the Jewish idiom, and they translated it this way in several scriptures (Mark 7:4; Luke 11:38; Hebrews 9:10). And Matthew 28:19 is another that could easily be translated as "washing" instead of "baptizing."

In chapter 3, we saw that in the Jewish idiom the phrase "in the name of" (such as in the scripture above) did not refer to a formula that was spoken aloud at baptisms (as was handed down from Rome); a set formula was not pictured in the prior Jewish history of water baptisms. Instead, "in the name of" referred to the authority and teaching relating to the one in whose name it was.

Since we already saw from Paul that the various water baptisms are no longer imposed, this scripture refers to the washing, cleansing, and sanctification that comes from receiving the truth of salvation through the Messiah, as well as the teaching that encompasses and is in the authority of "the Father and the Son and the Holy Spirit."

In Acts 19:3 when Paul finds certain disciples in Ephesus and they tell him they were baptized into John's baptism, it did not mean that John spoke a formula saying "I baptize you in the name of John" each time he baptized someone. There is no proof or history of any such concept.

In the Great Commission, the Messiah was teaching that they were to make disciples of all nations by spiritually baptizing/washing them **in the name of** (i.e., with all of the instruction and authority that comes from) the Father, Son, and Holy Spirit. He does not say anywhere in that verse or in any other scripture to water baptize anyone.

The Roman Church essentially focused on water baptism, using its own prescribed formula of spoken words, which Protestants would later come to dispute with their own formula. And why did Rome insist on this? Having authority over who would be water baptized gave the Church substantial control, even over kings and nations. Being filled with the Spirit of God was no longer emphasized, but outward religious ceremony and ritualistic observances were. The Messiah's baptism and Holy Spirit infilling were all but forgotten for approximately the next 1,700 to 1,800 years, until the early Pentecostal revivals began in the 1900s; the Spirit baptism and Spirit infilling have continued among various fellowships since then.

5.4 EARLY MESSIANIC JEWS DISPUTE THE ROMAN BAPTISM

A quick example of how Rome turned the focus back onto water baptism can be seen in how Roman theologians misinterpreted Paul's words below in reference to baptism:

> NAS Ephesians 4:5   one Lord, one faith, **one baptism,**

Rome summarily decided that Paul was referring to its water baptism when he spoke of "one baptism" in the scripture above. They did not consider Paul's teachings elsewhere, such as that Christ did not send him to baptize (1 Corinthians 1:17), and that Paul knew that the ritual washings of the law had been replaced with the Messiah's baptism for the New Covenant (Hebrews 9:10). Tertullian, called the father of Latin Christianity (i.e., Roman Catholicism), wrote the following around AD 180 in his treatise titled *On Baptism*:

> Happy is our sacrament of water, in that, by washing away the sins of our early blindness we are set free and admitted into eternal life! [29]

Later in his treatise, Tertullian loosely quotes the scripture above where Paul speaks of one baptism, and he applies it to the Roman water baptism:

> I know not whether any further point is mooted **to bring baptism into controversy**. Permit me to call to mind what I have omitted above, lest I seem to break off the train of impending thoughts in the middle. There is **to us one, and but one, baptism**; as well according to the Lord's gospel, as according to the apostles letters, inasmuch as he says, One God and one baptism, and one church in the heavens. [30]

In this context above, Tertullian is speaking out against a group of Messianic Jewish believers who teach against water baptism. It comes from a section with the heading, "Remarks on Heretical and Jewish Baptism," wherein he uses the trick of alienating Jewish Messianic believers by impugning other Jews who do not believe in the Messiah:

> But the Jewish Israel bathes daily, because he is daily being defiled… [31]

---

29   Roberts and Donaldson, *Ante-Nicene Fathers*, vol. 3, p. 669.
30   Roberts and Donaldson, *Ante-Nicene Fathers*, vol. 3, p. 676.
31   Roberts and Donaldson, *Ante-Nicene Fathers*, vol. 3, p. 676.

5. SPIRITUALLY WASHED, NOT BAPTIZED IN WATER 61

In Tertullian's previous chapter, he argues against these Jews (whom he often calls "heretics") and says that in their arguments against water baptism, they quote Paul's words that "Christ did not send me to baptize." However, these would not be unbelieving Jews quoting Paul against water baptism, since those Jewish leaders of Israel (mainly the Pharisees) still believed in their water baptisms. Instead, these are the remaining Jewish followers of the Messiah [32] who are not going along with Rome, who properly understand the Messiah's baptism, and know that water baptisms are no longer imposed by God. Tertullian writes how these Jews (who were speaking against Roman water baptism) were excommunicated from the Roman Church:

> Heretics, however, have no fellowship in our discipline, whom the mere fact of their excommunication testifies to be outsiders. [33]

This very interesting fact is worthy of further study—that a group of early Messianic believers existed who believed that water baptism was not required, and that this group was large enough that the renowned Roman theologian Tertullian felt he needed to write a treatise on water baptism to defend it. More on this subject is covered in chapter 6, where Tertullian quotes these Jewish believers appealing to Paul's words against water baptism.

5.5 CLEANING/WASHING THE OUTSIDE OF THE CUP

Earlier in this chapter, we saw that the original Greek text said that the Pharisee was bothered because Jesus did not first "baptize/wash" himself before the meal (Luke 11:38). But we did not show how Jesus responded, so here it is below:

---

[32] See my first book, *The Messianic Feast*, and the section titled "The Jewish Disconnect and the Fourteenthers" for that history, which is available here: http://themessianicfeast.com/wp-content/uploads/2015/01/TMF_SettingTable_1.pdf

[33] Roberts and Donaldson, *Ante-Nicene Fathers*, vol. 3, p. 676.

> NAS Luke 11:39 But the Lord said to him, "Now you Pharisees **clean the outside of the cup** and of the platter; but inside of you, you are full of robbery and wickedness.

We also saw this in Mark 7:4, where the Pharisees "baptized" cups, platters, and their hands to the wrist, among other water baptisms. Are we to believe that after Jesus rebukes the Pharisees for focusing on outward baptism (with water), he then essentially tells his disciples at the Great Commission to go out and baptize/wash the **outside** of people's cups, using water?

As was stated, in the Old Covenant John the Baptist said God sent him to baptize in **water**:

> NAS John 1:33 "And I did not recognize Him, but **He who sent me to baptize in water** said to me, 'He upon whom you see the Spirit descending and remaining upon Him, this is the one who baptizes in the Holy Spirit.'

In the New Covenant, Paul declared:

> NAS 1 Corinthians 1:17 For **Christ did not send me to baptize**, but to preach the gospel, not in cleverness of speech, that the cross of Christ should not be made void.

The pattern is clear. Paul, who taught that the various water baptisms were no longer imposed for those in the New Covenant (Hebrews 9:10 in Greek), said we are **baptized** by one *Spirit* (not by water):

> NAS 1 Corinthians 12:13 For **by one Spirit we were all baptized into one body**, whether Jews or Greeks, whether slaves or free, and we were all made to drink of one Spirit.

Paul says that we are washed and sanctified, not in water baptism but in the name of the Lord Jesus and in the Spirit of our God:

> NAS **1 Corinthians 6:11** And such were some of you; but **you were washed**, but **you were sanctified**, but you were justified **in the name of the Lord Jesus Christ, and in the Spirit of our God.**

> NAS **Titus 3:5** He saved us, **not on the basis of deeds which we have done** in righteousness, **but** according to His mercy, **by the washing of regeneration and renewing** by the Holy Spirit,

In Acts, chapter 19, when Paul comes across disciples in Ephesus, he assumes they are believers in the Messiah but discovers that they are disciples only of John. The first thing Paul is concerned with when he thinks that they already believe in the Messiah is **not** whether they were water baptized but if they had received the Holy Spirit when they believed:

> NAS **Acts 19:2** and he said to them, "**Did you receive the Holy Spirit when you believed?**" And they *said* to him, "No, we have not even heard whether there is a Holy Spirit."

Paul is a little taken back by their response, so he asks into what they were washed/baptized:

> NAS **Acts 19:3** And he said, "Into what then were you baptized?" And they said, "Into John's baptism."

So when Paul realizes they are disciples of John and not yet of the Messiah, he tells them that John's water baptism pointed forward to Jesus:

> NAS **Acts 19:4** And Paul said, "John baptized with the baptism of repentance, telling the people to believe in Him who was coming after him, that is, in Jesus."

And then when they understood this, they were baptized/washed by believing in the Messiah:

> NAS Acts 19:5 And when they heard this, they were baptized in the name of the Lord Jesus.

Most commentators assume that they were **water** baptized by Paul or someone else here; however, that is not what the scripture says. Protestants have used this verse against Catholics as proof that Paul is using the correct baptismal formula here, by supposedly **water** baptizing them in the name of the Lord Jesus, as opposed to the Catholic formula. But a proper formula for water baptism is not what this is saying. In 1 Corinthians, Paul said Christ did not send him to baptize and that he baptized only a few people. When he lists those few people that he baptized (Crispus, Gaius, and the house of Stephanas), he does not mention this group of disciples in Acts because Paul most likely did not **water** baptize them here. That's not what Christ sent Paul (or anyone else) to do, and it's not what Paul was concerned with.

Once they were "baptized/washed" by believing in the Messiah (verse 5 above), they were then ready to receive the gift of the Holy Spirit, which (as we saw) is what Paul wanted for them when he first met them (Acts 19:2). Right after they were spiritually washed by believing in the name of the Lord, they then received the Holy Spirit:

> NAS Acts 19:6 And when Paul had laid his hands upon them, the Holy Spirit came on them, and they *began* speaking with tongues and prophesying.

This portion of scripture in Acts 19 will be covered in more depth in chapter 9 of this book. And since we always want to view the scriptures in the proper context—the first-century Jewish perspective in which they were written—here is another verse to consider:

> NIV Mark 16:16 Whoever believes **and is baptized** will be saved, but whoever does not believe will be condemned.

Since Roman times, almost everyone has assumed this verse meant **water** baptism, but this does not say **water** baptized. Was the Messiah really going backward to John's baptism using water, or forward to the Spirit baptism he would provide in the New Covenant? The Roman Catholic Church chose not to picture this from the Jewish perspective. Instead, it interpreted it to mean that unless people were **water** baptized into the Roman Church using the correct formula of words, they could not be saved. As was mentioned earlier, this of course gave the Church great power and control.

However, in analyzing this verse from the first-century Messianic perspective of baptism, it makes far more sense to be saying, "He that believes and is washed will be saved," whereby the washing is simply the result of believing.

Some scholars believe that the verses from Mark 16:9–20 were an addition by a later scribe, even though they are present in 99 percent of the Greek manuscripts (just not two of the most respected ones). But for the purposes of this study, I will assume they are part of the original scripture.

It makes perfect sense that Mark 16:16 is referring to the same "washing" that the Great Commission scripture (Matthew 28:19) speaks about. We know that the Holy Spirit was the promise of the Father (Luke 24:49; Acts 1:4; 2:33) and that receiving it is a huge blessing. But being filled with the Holy Spirit is not required for salvation. We see that fact in various scriptures where those who are believers and are washed in the Messiah have not yet received the Holy Spirit infilling (Acts 8:5–16 and Acts 19:2). Mark speaks about the washing/baptism that one receives when becoming a believer, just as Paul does:

> ^{NAS} 1 Corinthians 6:11   And such were some of you; but **you were washed,** but you were sanctified, but you were justified in the name of the Lord Jesus Christ, **and in the Spirit of our God.**

Paul's focus was always on spiritual truth; he was not interested in returning to the ritual washings in water from the Old Covenant:

> NAS 1 Corinthians 12:13   For **by one Spirit** we were all **baptized** into one body, whether Jews or Greeks, whether slaves or free, and **we were all made to drink of one Spirit**.

Greek scholar and commentator R. C. H. Lenski demonstrated that the Greek word for baptism (*baptizo*) held a variety of meanings among the first-century Jews:

> Βαπτιζω, as all lexicographers agree, has a variety of meanings. It may refer to dip, immerse, wash, lave, sprinkle, cleanse, in fact, refer to the application of water in any form. This unquestioned fact is not altered by a reference to the original etymology, which is then limited to the meaning to immerse. The word must be understood in the sense that it had when Jesus spoke, and the New Testament shows conclusively that βαπτιζω was used to designate all manner of applications of water.[34]

However, if we only consider natural meanings, we can miss the fact that this word was also used spiritually, such as for the Messiah's spiritual baptism and for the washing that comes from believing in the Messiah, as we have seen. In the New Covenant, we were to move beyond these ritual washings in water and forward to the Messiah's Spirit baptism, not stay behind with ritual cleansings from the Law:

> NIV John 11:55   When it was almost time for the Jewish Passover, many went up from the country to Jerusalem **for their ceremonial cleansing before the Passover**.

> NAS John 2:6   Now there were six stone **waterpots** set there **for the Jewish custom of purification**, containing twenty or thirty gallons each.

---

34   Lenski, *The Interpretation of St. Matthew's Gospel*, pp. 1173–1174.

From the "baptism" of Elisha and Naaman (see chapter 2) to John's baptism and to these various ritual cleansings in water called baptisms in Christ's day, the Messiah's baptism would provide the spiritual washing that would fulfill them all (and also do away with the need and requirement for them).

> ^{NAS} Hebrews 9:10   since they *relate* only to food and drink and **various washings**,[35] regulations for the body imposed until a time of reformation.

Now we are ceremonially cleansed by receiving the word of God:

> ^{NAS} John 15:3   "You are already **clean** because of the word which I have spoken to you.

We are not cleansed and sanctified by ceremonial washing in water but by the spiritual washing that comes from the Lord and the word of God:

> ^{NAS} Ephesians 5:25–26   Husbands, love your wives, just as Christ also loved the church and gave Himself up for her; that He might **sanctify her**, having **cleansed** her by the **washing** of water **with the word**,

---

35 The "various washings" above is **baptisms** in the original Greek scripture.

6

A Closer Look: Why Did Paul Say Christ Did Not Send Me to Baptize?

"For I did not shrink from declaring to you the whole purpose of God."

— NAS Acts 20:27 —

Naturally, if all Bible commentators unwaveringly believe that water baptism is a requirement from God (and the Messiah), then they would need to somehow explain Paul's statements to the Corinthians. How do they explain his saying that Christ did not send him to baptize and that he even thanks God that he baptized only a few people?

In this chapter we will examine their explanations in greater detail, weigh them one by one in the light of all of the evidence, and see if their arguments hold water, so to speak. I believe that the baptism scriptures relating to Paul and how the commentators explain them are important enough to cover in its own chapter.

6.1 AT THE HEART: 1 CORINTHIANS

> NAS 1 Corinthians 1:14–15 **I thank God** that I **baptized none of you** except Crispus and Gaius, that no man should say you were baptized in my name.

If water baptism were a holy requirement from God (which some say is needed for salvation), why would Paul even say such a thing? Whatever is holding Paul back here, should he not just buckle down and do God's will? (Assuming, of course, that God requires water baptism.)

Some commentators look at the English words here (not considering the Jewish idioms) and say Paul was worried that some would say he baptized people using his own name in the formula (i.e., "I now baptize you in the name of Paul"). But if this were the real reason, what if some of the Corinthians were saying, "I was saved through Paul's preaching," and not giving the glory to God? Would this cause Paul to quit preaching the word of God and say, "I thank God I quit preaching and teaching, lest any of you take that wrong also"?

This is why it is so important to understand the Jewish idioms and in particular how they used the term "in the name of" as we saw in chapter 3. Just as when the disciples said they were baptized into John's baptism (Acts 19:3), it did not mean that John said "I now baptize you in the name of John" every time he water baptized. Indeed, this is not how the Jews baptized.

Nor did those who "were baptized unto Moses in the cloud and the sea" (1 Corinthians 10:2) employ a formula for a water baptism "in the name of Moses." This was not about Paul practicing an erroneous method of water baptism by using his own name instead of the name of Jesus. Rather, it was because Paul came to understand that the Old Covenant washings in water were no longer required in the New Covenant, and he didn't want people saying that they were **water** baptized under his authority or because of his teaching (i.e., "in his name").

This Corinthian fellowship originally began among some local Jews who resided in a house right next to the synagogue. Crispus was the synagogue leader, and many others there believed and were baptized/washed after they heard Paul's words concerning the Messiah:

> NAS Acts 18:8 And Crispus, the leader of the synagogue, believed in the Lord with all his household, and **many of the Corinthians** when they heard **were believing and being baptized**.

Although it says that many of the Corinthians were being baptized/washed, Paul states he water baptized only a few of them (1 Corinthians 1:14–17). I believe the reason Paul first water baptized a few of them, then stopped, is because the Lord revealed New Covenant truth to Paul; when Paul comprehended this, he completely halted doing water baptisms. He soon understood that water baptism was not imposed in the New Covenant (Hebrews 9:10) and that it was going back to Old Covenant ceremonial washings. Like Peter and the other disciples, Paul did not have full knowledge at the very beginning, but as God's Spirit led them, they all came into more truth just as the Messiah said would happen:

> NAS John 16:12–13 "I have **many more things to say to you, but you cannot bear** *them* **now**. "But when He, the Spirit of truth, comes, **He will guide you into all the truth**; for He will not speak on His own initiative, but whatever He hears, He will speak; and He will disclose to you what is to come.

> NAS John 14:26 "But the Helper, the Holy Spirit, whom the Father will send in My name, He will teach you all things, and **bring to your remembrance** all that I said to you.

After the Holy Spirit was poured out on the Gentiles, one defining change brought to Peter's "remembrance" was how Jesus had kept telling them the difference between his baptism and John's water baptism:

> NAS Acts 11:16 "And **I remembered** the word of the Lord, **how He used to say**, 'John baptized with water, **but** you shall be baptized with the Holy Spirit.'

Paul's words in First Corinthians are some of his strongest against water baptism, but he makes several other similar statements in other scriptures that we shall look at shortly. In looking at Paul's words again, we see that he **thanks God** he baptized only a few of them:

> NAS 1 Corinthians 1:14–15 **I thank God that I baptized none of you** except Crispus and Gaius, that no man should say you were baptized in my name.

It is critical to understand that Paul baptized only a few of the people in Corinth even though he was among them teaching for **18 months** (Acts 18:11):

> ^{NAS} Acts 18:8 And Crispus, the leader of the synagogue, believed in the Lord with all his household, and **many of the Corinthians** when they heard **were believing and being baptized.**

> ^{NAS} Acts 18:11 And he settled *there* **a year and six months**, teaching the word of God among them.

We have seen repeatedly that in their idiom, "baptized" (verse 8 above) can also refer to the "washing" that comes with believing, and that is most likely the case with verse 8. However, even if "baptized" refers to water baptism here, then Paul's abstaining is strong proof that he knew very early on that the Lord had moved beyond water baptisms. And that is the real reason he thanked God that he had baptized only a few of them over that eighteen-month period, and also why he said Christ **did not send me to baptize** (the supposed *water* baptism of the Great Commission notwithstanding).

6.2 THE COMMENTATORS WEIGH IN ON PAUL'S WORDS

With the commentators having inherited Roman theology on water baptism, they would need to explain why Paul would actually thank God for disobeying the Lord's commandment (assuming the Messiah meant *water* baptism in the Great Commission, Matthew 28:19–20). And they would also have to account for why Paul would say "Christ did not send me to baptize," since the Lord clearly told **the apostles** to baptize all nations (again assuming he meant *water* baptism).

As a side note, I am in no way trying to denigrate these commentators whose works have been a great help to me and who were good men of God. They are only defending a belief that they think is from the Lord but was actually handed down from Rome. I believe it's important to examine the truth on *water* baptism and that it was not what the Messiah taught or what he intended for the New Covenant, which is why I relate their comments here.

Regarding why Paul was not water baptizing people for those eighteen months in Corinth, the first explanation that commentators typically put forth is that he did not want people to think he was setting himself up as leader of a new sect by baptizing them with an improper formula and using his own name. We will look at their comments on verses 14 and 15 first:

> ᴺᴬˢ 1 Corinthians 1:14–15 **I thank God that I baptized none of you** except Crispus and Gaius, that no man should say you were baptized **in my name**.

Here is a brief synopsis of three well-known Bible commentators on this subject concerning these two scriptures:

1. Adam Clarke: "He was careful not to baptize, lest it should be supposed that he wished to make a party for himself; because superficial observers might imagine that he baptized them *into his own name*—to be his *followers*, though he baptized them into the name of Christ only." [36]

2. *Barnes' Notes* on verse 14: "To him it was now a subject of grateful reflection that he had *not* done it. He had not given any occasion for the suspicion that he had intended to set himself up as a leader of a sect or party." [37]

3. Jamieson, Fausset, and Brown: "**Baptizing was the office of the deacons** (Acts x.48); the apostles' office was to establish and superintend generally the churches. The deacons had more time for giving the necessary *instruction*

---

36 Clarke, *Clarke's Commentary*, vol. 3, p. 193 ("Romans to the Revelations" of vol. 2).
37 Barnes, *Barnes' Notes*, p. 678.

6. A Closer Look: Christ Did Not Send Me to Baptize 73

> *preparatory to baptism.* Crispus and Gaius, &c., being among the first converts, were baptized by Paul himself, who founded the church." [38]

If we look at Paul's statements in fuller context, these commentators' reasoning as to why Paul baptized only a few of them quickly breaks down:

> KJV 1 Corinthians 1:11–15 [11] For **it hath been declared unto me** of you, my brethren, **by them *which are of the house of Chloe*,** that there are contentions among you. [12] Now this I say, that every one of you saith, I am of Paul; and I of Apollos; and I of Cephas; and I of Christ. [13] Is Christ divided? was Paul crucified for you? or were ye baptized in the name of Paul? [14] **I thank God that I baptized none of you**, but Crispus and Gaius; [15] Lest any should say that I had baptized in mine own name.

Notice that Paul does not write, "I obviously knew of these contentions for the whole eighteen months I was with you, and that's why I water baptized only a few of you." No, that's not what Paul said.

In verse 11 above, Paul shows that he learns of these disputes **recently** from Chloe's household; Paul does not say that he knew this quarreling was happening for the eighteen months he was teaching them, and that this is why he baptized only a few of them. Since these contentions were a new thing and Paul only recently learned of them and their resulting schisms, it cannot be the real reason that Paul refused to water baptize so many Corinthians over that whole previous eighteen-month period. Thus, the commentators' explanation of Paul not wanting to create his own sect and his subsequent disobedience of the Lord's command to baptize all nations (in water) falls very short here.

---

38 Jamieson, Fausset, and Brown, *A Commentary*, vol. 3, p. 285 (part 3).

6.3 WHAT THE COMMENTATORS SAY ABOUT VERSES 16 AND 17

We will further explore why the prevailing teachings on verses 14 and 15 are not correct, but first let us look at what the commentators say concerning verses 16 and 17, where Paul goes further and even states that "Christ **did not send me to baptize**." Here, commentators essentially say that Paul believed that being an apostle was a higher-ranking office than what was required for doing water baptisms, and that those in inferior positions could handle that ministry.

> NAS 1 Corinthians 1:16–17   Now I did baptize also the household of Stephanas; beyond that, I do not know whether I baptized any other. **For Christ did not send me to baptize**, but to preach the gospel, not in cleverness of speech, that the cross of Christ should not be made void.

Here are their comments on those verses:

1. Adam Clarke: "It appears sufficiently evident that ***baptizing* was considered to be an *inferior* office**; and though every minister of Christ might administer it, yet apostles had more *important* work." [39]

2. *Barnes' Notes* on verse 17: "**It is probable that the business of baptism was entrusted to the ministers of the church of inferior talents**, or to those who were connected to the churches permanently, and not to those who were engaged chiefly in travelling from place to place." [40]

3. Jamieson, Fausset, and Brown: "He baptized some, **and would have baptized more**, but that his and the apostles' peculiar work was to preach the Gospel—to found, by

---

[39] Clarke, *Clarke's Commentary*, vol. 3, p. 193 ("Romans to the Revelations" of vol. 2).
[40] Barnes, *Barnes' Notes*, p. 679.

their autoptic testimony, particular churches, and
then to superintend the churches in general."[41]

Some of these explanations may sound plausible on the surface, but dig a little deeper and they quickly begin to fall apart.

As to the commentators' belief that Paul didn't baptize because he considered his office of apostle to be more dignified than to conduct water baptisms, leaving that rite to those in an "inferior office," we need only to look at the Messiah's directive.

The only scripture where the Messiah tells anyone to go baptize others (and he does not say **water** baptize) is what is known as the Great Commission, as we saw earlier:

> NAS Matthew 28:19-20 "Go therefore and make disciples of all the nations, **baptizing them** in the name of the Father and the Son and the Holy Spirit, teaching them to observe all that I commanded you; and lo, I am with you always, even to the end of the age."

In previous chapters, we have noted that the Messiah was not going backward to the ritual washings in water in his instructions here. Rather, he was moving forward to the baptism that was promised by God (John 1:33), by himself (Acts 1:5), by John the Baptist (Matthew 3:11; Mark 1:8; Luke 3:16), and by Peter (Acts 11:16). This was the Messiah's Spirit baptism.

But, for the sake of argument, it must be understood that Jesus is telling **the apostles** to go out and baptize all the nations. So if the Messiah actually meant to go backward to an Old Covenant *water* baptism (except in his name) instead of forward to the Spirit baptism that he brought in, he does not tell the apostles to have their underlings do it, he tells **them** to do it. If the Messiah tells the apostles to go out water baptizing everyone, should Paul first submit but then make excuses as to why he should be left out of this all-important rite?

---

[41] Jamieson, Fausset, and Brown, *A Commentary*, vol. 3, p. 285 (part 3).

If "Christ did not send me to baptize" means what the commentators say (that the position of apostle was above performing baptisms), then why didn't the Messiah explain that to the apostles when he told them to go out and supposedly water baptize the nations? He could have said, "Go and *water* baptize all nations, but don't you personally do it, for you are more high-level people—get those of a lower rank to fulfill this menial ministry."

We have no record anywhere that the Messiah ever said such a thing. If Matthew 28:19 was truly in the original scripture, then Jesus told **the apostles** to go and baptize all the nations, and that meant the apostles were not exempt from this duty (in the way he wanted, of course, with his Spirit baptism). Nothing in that statement says for the apostles to go find some lower-level people to perform baptisms while they sit on the sidelines.

Additionally, wouldn't this belief of the commentators be opposite of what Jesus taught the apostles at the Last Supper—that they should be humble enough to wash one another's feet? So how much more to water baptize, if that were indeed God's command?

Now if Paul were trying to dissuade people from following him or from setting himself up as a great one to follow, then in theory, speaking about his lofty position is the worst thing he could have done. According to the commentators, Paul said these things because he was of a more worthy office than to spend time water baptizing. So, are we really to believe this assumption that instead of humbling himself before any who would want to follow him and create a new sect, he exalts his office over others so they won't want to follow him after all?

This, of course, makes no sense.

Additionally, the Messiah declared that no prophet was greater than John the Baptist, and after all, John didn't think water baptism was below his office when God told him to go do it (John 1:33). So is Paul really thinking of himself as far greater than John the Baptist, that Paul cannot take a day or two to water baptize all of the Corinthians?

And if Paul were genuinely worried that a new sect who followed him might be created, should he have not given up preaching too, because those who believed and were saved might say they got saved by him, thus causing him to be the focus? Also, that he should give up praying for anyone to be healed, for they might then proclaim they were healed by Paul, causing even more contentions? So actually, getting completely out of the ministry was the only thing Paul could do to avoid all of these problems.

In circling back, should not all pastors and priests today also follow Paul's example and give up water baptism, since someone might say that Pastor Smith or Priest Jones baptized them in their own name?

The commentators' explanations do not pass the test of scriptural scrutiny here. The only thing that makes sense is that, in the Great Commission, the Messiah was not going backward to the Old Covenant water baptisms. And Paul knew this.

Paul understood the revelation that the Messiah had moved beyond John's water baptism to his own promised Spirit baptism, just as God revealed to John the Baptist:

> NAS John 1:33 "And I did not recognize Him, but **He who sent me to baptize in water** said to me, 'He upon whom you see the Spirit descending and remaining upon Him, **this is the one who baptizes in the Holy Spirit.**'

> NAS Mark 1:8 "I baptized you with water; **but** He will baptize you with the Holy Spirit."

Just as Jesus also had said the same on various occasions, as Peter here relates:

> NAS Acts 11:16 "And I remembered the word of the Lord, **how He used to say,** 'John baptized with water, **but** you shall be baptized with the Holy Spirit.'

Paul therefore did not want his name connected to doing water baptisms, which is why he thanked God he had not continued doing them, because Christ did not send him to do them. Paul was instead focused on the Messiah's true teaching—on getting people baptized/washed and filled with the Holy Spirit (Acts 19:2; 1 Corinthians 12:13; Ephesians 5:18)—because he knew this was the Messiah's directive. This was the same directive the Lord Jesus gave to the prophet Ananias when Paul was coming to know the Lord, to get Paul filled with the Holy Spirit:

> ^{NAS} Acts 9:17 And Ananias departed and entered the house, and after laying his hands on him said, "Brother Saul, the Lord Jesus, who appeared to you on the road by which you were coming, has sent me **so that you may regain your sight, and be filled with the Holy Spirit.**"

And here when the risen Messiah sends Ananias to pray that Paul be filled with the Holy Spirit, he does not say, "Oh, and I almost forgot, be sure to get Paul water baptized also, using the correct formula, for this rite is very important."

6.4 ANALYZING HEBREWS 9:10

We covered that when Paul first ministered in Corinth, he did initially water baptize a few people, but he quickly discerned that by doing so, he was going back to the Old Covenant washings. And as we saw in his First Corinthians letter, he understood that Christ had not sent him to baptize. And he certainly understood that water baptism regulations were no longer imposed when he wrote to the Hebrews. Here again are two different translations of verse 10:

> ^{NAB} Hebrews 9:9–10 This is a symbol of the present time, in which gifts and sacrifices are offered that cannot perfect the worshiper in conscience but only in matters of food and drink and **various ritual washings**: regulations concerning the flesh, **imposed until** the time of the new order.

> ^{YLT} Hebrews 9:10 only in victuals, and drinks, and **different baptisms**, and **fleshly ordinances**—till the time of reformation **imposed** upon *them*.

I give a second translation above (Young's Literal Translation) for verse 10 because it is more accurate to the original Greek by translating the Greek word "*baptismos*" as "baptisms" instead of "ritual washings." Now, if we are not programmed by history to think of the rite of water baptism each time we see this Greek word for baptism/washing, this is not a problem. But I add this because I want to make it clear that Paul uses the Greek word for baptism here when he speaks of the Old Covenant washings that are no longer imposed. We have somewhat glossed over this verse in other chapters, but this is one of Paul's strongest statements against water baptism, so let us look at this a little closer.

Only a few "different baptisms" existed in Paul's day, so what baptisms are Paul referring to here that are no longer "imposed"? We know the Messiah's baptism (the Spirit baptism) is still in effect, because that is the **one baptism** that Paul explains is still God's will:

> NAS Ephesians 4:5   one Lord, one faith, **one baptism,**

Paul makes it clear in various scriptures that the **one baptism** he is concerned about is the Messiah's Spirit baptism:

> NAS 1 Corinthians 12:13   For **by one Spirit** we were all **baptized** into one body, whether Jews or Greeks, whether slaves or free, and we were all made to drink of one Spirit.

The baptisms (ritual washings) that Paul said were no longer imposed were **not** the *water* baptisms that were traditions of the Pharisees (who baptized cups and pots as well as the hands to the wrist before eating bread, as cited in Mark 7:2–8 in Greek). Those specific baptisms were never required by God, so it cannot be those baptisms:

> YLT Mark 7:4   and, *coming* from the market-place, if they do not **baptize themselves**, they do not eat; and many other things there are that they received to hold, **baptisms** of cups, and pots, and brazen vessels, and couches.

The only water baptisms imposed by God were various Temple baptisms and John's baptism, but the only baptism to actually be continued was the Messiah's Spirit baptism:

> NAS Matthew 3:11 "As for me, **I baptize you with water** for repentance, **but** He who is coming after me is mightier than I, and I am not fit to remove His sandals; **He will baptize you with the Holy Spirit** and fire.

The Messiah's baptism is the "one baptism" that Paul understood was now in effect, since Old Covenant water baptisms were no longer imposed or needed. As for New Covenant believers, neither God nor Jesus ever said to *water* baptize anyone. Yes, some scriptures show the apostles (even Paul) sometimes got involved in performing water baptisms, but these verses must be interpreted with the knowledge and history we have gained from our previous chapters. In fact, when we study various baptism scriptures, the following points must be kept in mind:

1. The apostles were all coming into new truth as the Holy Spirit was leading them, just as the Messiah promised would happen (John 16:12, 13). One example is in Acts 10, where Peter comes to understand that in the New Covenant, the believing (uncircumcised) Gentiles are not to be viewed as common or unclean.

2. We also saw from the clear history in the previous chapters that just because the word "baptize" was used, it did not mean literal **water** baptism; in the natural-to-spiritual idiom common in the day, it often referred to the spiritual washing that comes when one believes. To say they were "baptized in the name of Jesus" can easily mean they were washed from their sins by receiving and believing in the spiritual washing provided by the Messiah. We saw in the two sections that covered the Jewish phrase "in

the name of" (3.6 and 3.7) that to the Jews, this was only pointing out the **focus and authority** that something was done in, not the rigidly prescribed formula as Rome misunderstood. When the scripture says, "But as many as received Him, to them He gave the right to become children of God, *even* to those who **believe in His name**" (John 1:12, NAS), it is not referring to a magical type of belief in a name.

After all, the name Jesus always went by was not the English word "Jesus," but his Greek name pronounced *ee-ay-sooce*, so if the intent is a rigid belief in his actual name, we have all missed it. The name "Jesus" did not come into being until English translators added the "J" to it around AD 1500, so if believing in his actual name was the key, then we have all fallen short there, too. Instead, what it means is that we believe in the person of the Messiah—who he was and who he is, how he fulfilled God's plan, how he manifested God's nature to us, and all of the truth and teaching he brought forth. This is what believing "in his name" or baptizing "in his name" meant in the Jewish idiom (as covered in chapter 3). "Baptized in his name" meant receiving the baptism/washing that the Messiah brought forth, the spiritual washing that he provides.

3. One more aspect is that since Messianic believers were constantly meeting in the Temple, (where ritual baths/baptisms for purification were always required before entering), some scriptures may be showing this first-century Temple requirement being satisfied (Acts 21: 26, etc.).

4. We have also seen Jewish rules concerning the proselyte, wherein baptism in water was required for the Gentile to ritually wash away any idolatry and to be accepted into the Jewish nation. This is almost certainly what

Peter means when, concerning the Gentiles whom God had filled with the Holy Spirit, he says, "Surely no one can refuse **the water** for these to be baptized who have received the Holy Spirit just as we *did*, can he?" (Acts 10:47). When he says "**the** water," it refers to a specific water—the water baptism required for a proselyte, as we saw in chapter 2. According to Jewish first-century religious law, believing Gentiles could be accepted into the Jewish commonwealth only after a water baptism.

Paul knew that doing these "deeds" of the law like circumcision and various water baptisms is not how purification or salvation comes in the New Covenant:

> NAS Titus 3:5   He saved us, **not on the basis of deeds which we have done** in righteousness, **but** according to His mercy, **by the washing of regeneration and renewing by the Holy Spirit,**

6.5   THE INFLUENCE OF TERTULLIAN AND THE JEWISH DISCONNECT

It is interesting to note that some of the points of dispute covered in this chapter were also debated 1,800 years ago. Let's look at a few quotes concerning baptism from a Roman-based Bible commentator who lived around AD 155–240, one who was mentioned earlier in chapter 5.

As Rome took over the Church and Jewish understandings and influences were pushed out, Roman theologians became the required voices to listen to and obey. One of these earliest commentators was Tertullian, the son of a Roman centurion. Tertullian was considered the father of Latin Christianity (i.e., Rome). He authored a very early writing (around AD 200) explaining the Roman doctrine of the ritual of Communion and an early version of transubstantiation. In the following passage, he refers to people needing to make the sign of the cross and no longer being allowed to handle their own bread and wine in their Eucharist ritual, lest some of the Lord's body fall to the ground:

> It was heretofore tolerated in some places that communicants should take each one his portion, with his own hand, **but now we suffer none to receive this sacrament except at the hand of the minister**... We are concerned if even a particle of the wine or bread, made ours, in the Lord's Supper, falls to the ground, by our carelessness. In all the ordinary occasions of life we furrow our foreheads with the sign of the Cross, in which we glory none the less because it is regarded as our shame by the heathen in presence of whom it is a profession of our faith. [42]

In other words, he was instrumental in promoting doctrines that were no longer connected to first-century Jewish understandings. In his writings, Tertullian has a whole treatise on the importance of water baptism, even stating that one cannot be saved without it. This quote comes from his chapter titled, "Of the Necessity of Baptism for Salvation":

> "When, however, the prescript is laid down that **'without baptism, salvation is attainable by none'** (chiefly on the ground of that declaration of the Lord, who says, 'Unless one be born of water, he hath not life.' "), there arise immediately scrupulous, nay rather audacious, doubts on the part of some..." [43]

He wrote this entire chapter on water baptism to argue against those in his day (Messianic Jewish believers) who were saying **water baptism is no longer imposed**. This debate between these parties was occurring right at the time of the main theological battles between Rome and those holding to more Jewish beliefs. Rome, as the reigning world power, was methodically refusing Jewish Messianic beliefs, rejecting their understandings, and calling all Jews heretics, including Jewish believers in the Messiah (see the chapter titled "The Jewish Disconnect and the Fourteenthers" in my book, *The Messianic Feast*, for this history).

---

42 Roberts and Donaldson, *Ante-Nicene Fathers*, vol. 3, p. 103.
43 Roberts and Donaldson, *Ante-Nicene Fathers*, vol. 3, pp. 674–675. (Concerning John 3:1–8)

That same chapter shows that Tertullian did the same things as the soon-to-be Roman emperor Constantine would later attempt—to lump all Jews together (believers and unbelievers) as apostates to strengthen their Roman theological positions. Tertullian opens his baptism treatise by speaking against the "heretics" who said baptism was no longer required, calling them of the "Cainite heresy." He thus rejects and impugns all Jews (who in his belief were like Cain, who slew his brother) as being like those relative few who pushed for the Messiah's death.

This was a straw man argument against Jewish believers. Emperor Constantine did the same thing years later in the debates concerning Jewish believers who honored the Lord Jesus by keeping the 14th day Passover in a special way (they knew that he was actually crucified on this day of Passover). Predictably, the Roman Church did not like these Jewish practices and instead wanted to celebrate Roman Easter on Sunday. Here is Constantine's quote in his decree to all of the churches:

> By rejecting their custom, we establish and hand down to succeeding ages one which is more reasonable, and which has been observed ever since the day of our Lord's sufferings. Let us, then, have nothing in common with the Jews, who are our adversaries. For we have received from our Saviour another way. A better and more lawful line of conduct is inculcated by our holy religion. Let us with one accord walk therein, my much-honoured brethren, studiously avoiding all contact with that evil way.[44]

Here is more from Tertullian as he rails against Jewish believers who said Abraham pleased God by faith and not by doing the "sacrament" of water baptism:

> Here, then, those miscreants provoke questions. And so **they say, "Baptism is not necessary for them to whom faith is**

---

[44] Schaff and Wace, *Nicene and Post-Nicene Fathers*, vol. 3, p. 47.

sufficient; for withal, Abraham pleased God by a sacrament of no water, but of faith."[45]

Tertullian argues against their statement that salvation is by faith instead of by doing the deed of water baptism:

> **For the *law* of baptizing has been *imposed*, and the formula prescribed**: "Go," *He* saith, "teach the nations, baptizing them into the name of the Father, and of the Son, and of the Holy Spirit."[46]

He continues arguing against this supposed "Cainite" heresy:

> "But they roll back *an objection* from *that* apostle himself, in that he said, 'For Christ sent me not to baptize;" **as if by this argument baptism were done away!** For if so, why did he baptize Gaius, and Crispus, and the house of Stephanas? However, even if Christ had not sent him to baptize, yet He had given other apostles the precept to baptize. But these words were written to the Corinthians in regard of the circumstances of that particular time; seeing that schisms and dissensions were agitated among them, while one attributes everything to Paul, another to Apollos. For which reason the 'peacemaking' apostle, for fear he should seem to claim all gifts for himself, says that he had been sent 'not to baptize, but to preach.' For preaching is the prior thing, baptizing the posterior. Therefore the preaching came first: but I think baptizing withal was lawful to him to whom preaching was."[47]

Do some of these arguments sound familiar?

---

45 Roberts and Donaldson, *Ante-Nicene Fathers*, vol. 3, pp. 675–676.
46 Roberts and Donaldson, *Ante-Nicene Fathers*, vol. 3, p. 676.
47 Roberts and Donaldson, *Ante-Nicene Fathers*, vol. 3, p. 676.

7

A Closer Look:
But Peter Said Baptism Saves You

It seems that with most major Bible doctrines, there are always one or two verses that just don't seem to fit in with established truth from other scriptures. This sometimes stems from translation issues or from not understanding the idioms in which the scripture was written. Or, in rare cases, it results from the scripture being a later addition of spurious content that was not in the original Greek documents (such as portions of 1 John 5:7–8).

One major rule of hermeneutics (Bible interpretation) is that you do not allow one or two verses to overturn the main body of truth that is clear from many other scriptures. Instead, you consider if those one or two odd scriptures can be interpreted so they harmonize with well-established truth from the whole Bible. The transition from Greek scriptures to English is not always easy, and certain idioms and nuances do not always come straight across in the translations.

My first book solved the 1,800-year-old controversy on whether the Last Supper was the Passover (or whether Jesus was instead crucified on this 14th day Passover). In it were three scriptures that proved especially difficult: Matthew 26:17, Mark 14:12, and Luke 22:7. One book chapter listed over 50 reasons why the Last Supper could not possibly have been the Passover, yet the English translations of these three verses *seemed* to make it obvious that Jesus was not crucified at the Passover (i.e., at the proper legal time) but instead ate the legal Passover during the previous night at the Last Supper.

This controversy was solved by correctly translating those three verses using the accepted rules for Greek grammar as they were intended in the original Greek by the Jewish believers who wrote them (see the chapter titled "The Three Major Greek Keys That Unlock the Gospels" in *The Messianic Feast*). This in turn shed light on the doctrine called the Blessed Eucharist, showing that it originated in Rome and was not taught by the Messiah or early Jewish disciples.

As with the previous chapter concerning Paul, this one will explore in greater detail the verses in First Peter, in which baptism is mentioned but have been misinterpreted over the centuries as something quite different than originally intended.

7.1 PETER AND THE "WASHING" THAT SAVES US

As for explaining whether the Lord wants water baptism or his own Spirit baptism, the most difficult verse is 1 Peter 3:21, where Peter really *seems* to say that baptism **in water** is what saves you. Yet, we will soon see that harmonizing this verse with the main body of evidence ends up being fairly easy. Here is that portion of scripture:

> NAS 1 Peter 3:20-21 who once were disobedient, when the patience of God kept waiting in the days of Noah, during the construction of the ark, in which a few, that is, **eight persons, were brought safely through** *the* **water. And corresponding to that, baptism now saves you—not the removal of dirt from the flesh, but an appeal to God for a good conscience—through the resurrection of Jesus Christ,**

The first thing to notice is that Peter does not say that it is *water* baptism that saves you. So we would then need to determine if Peter intended the baptism/washing **in water** (that Paul says is no longer imposed in the New Covenant), or whether he meant the **Spirit** baptism that Jesus provides is what now saves us. Here is what Paul wrote to the Hebrews:

> NIV Hebrews 9:9 This is an illustration for the present time, indicating that the gifts and sacrifices being offered **were not able to clear the conscience of the worshiper.**

NAB Hebrews 9:10   but only in matters of food and drink and **various ritual washings**: regulations concerning the flesh, **imposed until** the time of the new order.

Remember that the words translated above as "various ritual washings" are actually "various **baptisms**" in the original Greek. We also know that Paul thanked God that he water baptized only a few people, and then he stated emphatically that Christ did not send him to baptize. This, of course, is very bizarre for Paul to say if water baptism is actually what saves us. And so Paul would thus be saying elsewhere to the Corinthians, "I thank God I got only a couple of you saved by water baptism, because Christ did not send me to save anyone."

7.2   REASONS WHY PETER DOES NOT MEAN THAT BAPTISM *IN WATER* SAVES US

Before we see what Peter is saying and meaning here, let's first show what he is *not* intending.

Some may say that Peter is picturing Noah being saved by a water baptism and that this corresponds to the Catholic/Protestant **water** baptism that saves us. That idea breaks down when we consider the facts. For instance, those saved under Noah were never water baptized—they remained dry in the ark. The only ones who could be said to be water baptized (meaning "washed/immersed" in Greek) were those who drowned in the flood.

As I mentioned earlier, one of the rules for proper Bible interpretation says that we do not allow one slightly cryptic verse to overturn well-established Bible truth. So with that in mind, please consider the following facts that prove Peter does not mean that baptism **in water** is what saves us:

1. If baptism in water is what really saves us, couldn't the Messiah, the savior of the world, have told us just once to specifically *water* baptize, so we could know how to be saved? In all of the Messiah's teachings, not once does he

ever tell anyone to be baptized *in water*. Not only that, but he tells the unbaptized thief on the cross that he will soon be with him in Paradise, instead of explaining to him that without a proper water baptism he cannot be saved.

2. Also, why is it that Jesus (Acts 1:5), God (John 1:33), John the Baptist (Matthew 3:11, Mark 1:8, and Luke 3:18), and even Peter (Acts 11:16) all point forward to the Messiah's Spirit baptism, if it is really the one in water that saves us? Every time, they clearly contrast the two baptisms, saying that John baptized in water *but* the Messiah will **baptize in the Holy Spirit**. The scripture states specifically that it was God who sent John to baptize in water (John 1:33), but not a single scripture exists where God sends the Messiah to baptize **in water**.

3. And why on earth does Paul boast that he baptized only a few people, even saying that Christ did not send him to baptize, if baptism in water saves us? Doesn't he want people saved? Shouldn't Paul's priority be getting people saved, and not (as the commentators said) feeling that his office was too high for such mundane things?

4. And, as we saw above, why then does Paul say that the washings/baptisms from the Old Covenant are carnal ordinances that are no longer imposed on New Covenant believers if water baptism saves us? (Hebrews 9:10)

5. And why then does Paul say there is **one baptism** (Ephesians 4:5), showing in several scriptures that this one baptism was the Spirit baptism (1 Corinthians 6:11, 12:13, etc.)? If there are clearly two baptisms (the water baptism that supposedly saves us and the Messiah's Spirit baptism that apparently is not effective for salvation), why would Paul say there is one?

6. If water baptism saves us, then that would have God pouring out the Holy Spirit on unsaved people (Acts 10:44–48) who had not yet been water baptized (verse 48). And does God fill unsaved people (i.e., not water baptized) with His spirit? No, the truth is that they were saved and washed by believing and were thus ready for God to infill them with His spirit without a water baptism. Are we really going to say that these people can believe in the Messiah for salvation, be washed by his blood, and then be filled with God's Holy Spirit, and yet still they need a dipping in water with the correct formula of words spoken over them by a priest, pastor, or rabbi to be saved?

7. Paul said the Messiah saves us, not because of any **deeds which we have done** (deeds you perform, such as circumcision or **water baptism**), but "according to His mercy, by the **washing** (of regeneration and renewing) **by the Holy Spirit**" (Titus 3:5).

8. Paul also wrote that we are saved by believing the truth and by the sanctifying work of the spirit, not by water washing:

> NIV 2 Thessalonians 2:13 But we ought always to thank God for you, brothers loved by the Lord, because from the beginning **God chose you to be saved through the sanctifying work of the Spirit** and through belief in the truth.

9. And if Peter is really saying that baptism in water saves us, couldn't he have stated the correct formula to be spoken at the rite, lest many be lost by not getting that part accurate? Also, Peter teaches elsewhere that forgiveness comes to everyone who believes in the Messiah (Acts 10:43), not to those who have undergone the rite of water baptism.

10. And if water baptism saves us, why then does the Lord Jesus specifically tell Ananias to go pray and get Paul filled with the Holy Spirit but says nothing about water baptizing Paul to get him saved? (Acts 9:17).

7.3   THE SIMPLE ANSWER FOR 1 PETER 3:21

Again, because this verse does not specifically say that **water** baptism saves you, we therefore need to determine whose baptism Peter is referring to. Considering all of the proofs we have examined, it should be clear that the Messiah's Holy Spirit baptism is what is effectual in the New Covenant and that various water baptisms are no longer imposed. The rules of hermeneutics say we cannot overturn all of these scriptural facts with one cryptic verse. Instead, we see how this verse can be properly translated and understood to fit in with the rest of the established truth seen elsewhere (as laid out in this book).

The first important thing to know in verse 21 below is that the Greek word translated as "corresponding to" is actually "antitype" in Greek (*antitupos*[48]). We see in the scriptures that there are types and antitypes that "correspond to" each other. For instance, we often hear that the Passover lamb was a "type" of Christ in that it pointed forward to him. We also saw many types and antitypes in the natural-to-spiritual chapter.

Perhaps the following sentence better expresses what Peter intends here: The *natural* example of Noah coming safely through the flood **corresponds to** the *spiritual* baptism that the Messiah provides and that now saves us.

---

48   In Bible college, we were taught the same meanings for "type" and "antitype" that Theopedia.com expresses here: "Typology is a method of biblical interpretation whereby an element found in the Old Testament is seen to prefigure one found in the New Testament. The initial one is called the *type* and the fulfillment is designated the *antitype*." (Adapted from Theopedia.com, s.v. "Biblical typology.") That definition was used in my first book. However, I have come to the understanding that this is not always correct, based on verse 21 here and also Hebrews 9:24, where the Greek word "antitype" is used, which says that the manmade holy place is the antitype of the real one in heaven. And of course, using the previous definition, the manmade place should be the type and the true holy place in heaven the antitype. Therefore, the more accurate definition for antitype is what *BDAG Lexicon* lists, which is "corresponding to" (as NAS also translates it in their translation of 1 Peter 3:21).

And using the proper rules of Greek grammar, let's consider this scripture from the NAS translation below, but with a few words added (by me) in brackets and in italics to help demonstrate what Peter is expressing:

> NAS 1 Peter 3:21   And **corresponding to** that, baptism now saves you—not the [*water baptism that is merely the*] removal of dirt from the flesh, but [*the Messiah's Spirit baptism that is*] an appeal to God for a good conscience—through the resurrection of Jesus Christ,

(Note that translators often add certain words—usually in italics—to give proper nuance when going from Greek to English, and the practice is perfectly fine as long as it helps clarify what the writer meant. That is why I added these italicized words in brackets.)

In his excellent book, *Greek Grammar Beyond the Basics*, Greek scholar Daniel B. Wallace shows that translating this Greek as written above is within the sphere of intended meaning. He does not give his statement below as an argument against water baptism but simply explains the Greek construction in this verse:

> The Semantic force of this sentence is: "And baptism now saves you. **I'm not talking about the kind which removes dirt from the body…**"[49]

The kind of baptism that removes dirt from the body is of course water baptism (and only water baptism), but Peter specifically states here that this is **not** the baptism that will save you. Peter is instead saying in verse 21 that it is the Messiah's baptism/washing that saves us—by our believing in and appropriating the atonement he provided for us through his death and resurrection.

Peter is saying that the example of Noah and those who obeyed God's plan in building the ark is the antitype of (i.e., corresponds to)

---

[49] Wallace, *Greek Grammer Beyond the Basics*, p. 119.

those who accept the Messiah's Spirit baptism and follow the New Covenant plan of God, which "now saves us."

After his ascension, the Messiah brought in the Spirit baptism that was promised by God (John 1:33, Luke 24:49, and Acts 2:33), by himself (Acts 1:5), by John the Baptist (Matthew 3:11, Mark 1:8, and Luke 3:16), and mentioned by Peter (Acts 11:16). This is the true baptism/washing that Peter says is an appeal to God for a good conscience.

In Hebrews 9:9–10 (in 7.1 above), Paul explains that animal sacrifices and **water baptisms** could **not** make the worshippers perfect **in conscience**. A few verses later, Paul states the only thing that can truly cleanse our conscience:

> NAS Hebrews 9:14 **how much more will the blood of Christ**, who through the eternal Spirit offered Himself without blemish to God, **cleanse your conscience** from dead works to serve the living God?

When Peter speaks of the baptism (verse 21 further above) that is an "appeal to God for **a good conscience**," he therefore has to be referring to the Messiah's Spirit baptism. Also, since neither God nor Jesus ever said to specifically **water** baptize anyone in the New Covenant, it makes much more sense that it is the Messiah's Spirit baptism that saves us, not any of the water baptisms that are no longer imposed.

7.4 MORE ON WHY PETER MENTIONS NOAH

If the explanation is correct here (for 1 Peter 3:21), then why does Peter bring in the Noah example and say it corresponds to our baptism? Perhaps another answer is partly found in the original Greek here and partly by understanding the Jewish idioms. When most Christians think of baptism, what comes to mind is an 1,800-year-old tradition with a formula to be spoken over the recipient (that originated in Rome and then changed with the Protestants). The Jews in Christ's day did not have this picture.

For instance, when Paul says they were baptized into Moses in the cloud and the sea, this does not really equate with the Catholic/Protestant picture of baptism:

> ^{NAS} 1 Corinthians 10:1-2   For I do not want you to be unaware, brethren, that our fathers were all under the cloud, and all passed through the sea; and all were **baptized** into Moses **in the cloud and in the sea;**

This was not Moses saying to the people, "I now baptize you in the name of Moses," using a certain formula, for they all remained dry when they went through the Red Sea. It does not really equate with the Catholic/Protestant picture of baptism. But when we picture this through first-century Jewish eyes, this fits with the Old Covenant washings that were passing from an unclean state (idolatry in Egypt) to a sanctified one where they were set apart to God. Paul is picturing what happened with them leaving Egypt as a spiritual washing that points forward to our spiritual washing.

Peter, like Paul, may be using a similar example. And if Peter is referring to Noah and those in the ark as a baptism, and that this "corresponds to" the Messiah's Spirit baptism in the New Covenant, it is in the same sense that Paul refers to those following Moses in the cloud and the sea being a baptism. Peter would thus be contrasting Noah's baptism/washing to the Messiah's Spirit baptism "that now saves you," just like John the Baptist and Jesus often contrasted, and just as Peter remembered:

> ^{NAS} Acts 11:16   "And I remembered the word of the Lord, how He used to say, 'John baptized **with water, but you** shall be **baptized** with the Holy Spirit.'

In other words, those with Noah were saved, spiritually washed, and sanctified to God by believing and following His plan. Peter uses that to point forward to the Spirit baptism, the one baptism/washing (Ephesians 4:5) that Paul taught on:

7. A Closer Look: But Peter Said Baptism Saves You   95

ᴺᴬˢ 1 Corinthians 12:13   For **by one Spirit we were all baptized** into one body, whether Jews or Greeks, whether slaves or free, and we were all made to drink of one Spirit.

One more aspect of the Greek helps point this out. The Greek word for baptism in verse 21 (below) is *anarthrous* (meaning that it has no article), so, therefore, it could be translated here as either "baptism" or "a baptism." We have changed it to "a baptism" in the NAS translation below because that's perfectly legal according to the rules for Greek grammar and because this very well may be what Peter is getting at here. As with the earlier example, we have again added the italicized words in brackets to this translation to give the sense of what Peter may mean; we also want to remember that to the Jews the Greek word for baptism often meant washing:

ᴺᴬˢ 1 Peter 3:21   And corresponding to that, [*a*] **baptism** [*i.e., a spiritual "washing"*] now saves you—not the [*water baptism that is merely the*] removal of dirt from the flesh, but [*the Messiah's Spirit baptism that is*] an appeal to God for a good conscience—through the resurrection of Jesus Christ,

ᴳᴺᵀ 1 Peter 3:21   ὃ καὶ ὑμᾶς ἀντίτυπον νῦν σῴζει βάπτισμα, οὐ σαρκὸς ἀπόθεσις ῥύπου ἀλλὰ συνειδήσεως ἀγαθῆς ἐπερώτημα εἰς θεόν, δι' ἀναστάσεως Ἰησοῦ Χριστοῦ,

As previously mentioned, translators often add certain words for clarity when going from one language to another. And there is nothing wrong with this if it helps explain what the original writer was meaning.

Just as Paul equated the passing through the cloud and the sea with Moses as baptism, Peter also seems to picture the passing through the water with Noah as baptism. And he says, "corresponding to that, **a baptism** now saves you, not the…," and Peter then lets them know that he does not mean the water baptisms/washings of the Old Covenant under which these Jewish believers had grown up with, but the baptism that gives a good conscience because of the Messiah finishing his atoning work and being raised from the dead.

This was actually a common Jewish usage of the word "baptism"; it was sometimes used to indicate a sort of passage from an unclean to a sanctified state, or from one phase or realm to another. When the Messiah spoke of the baptism that he would undergo, he was not referring to a baptism in water but to the fiery trial into which he would be immersed:

> NAS Mark 10:38–39 But Jesus said to them, "You do not know what you are asking for. Are you able to drink the cup that I drink, or to **be baptized with the baptism with which I am baptized**?" And they said to Him, "We are able." And Jesus said to them, "The cup that I drink you shall drink; and you shall be baptized with the baptism with which I am baptized.

And in Luke:

> NAB Luke 12:50 There is **a baptism** with which I must be **baptized**, and how great is my anguish until it is accomplished!

Peter may also have been subtly referring to this same fiery trial aspect, connecting what those who followed Noah endured to the "baptism" of persecution that Peter's intended readers are experiencing (see 1 Peter 3:14–20 that leads up to our verse 21).

Peter would also have known the Lord's teaching, where he compares the days of Noah (Matthew 24:37–39) to those who are part of the promised rapture. There, in the Greek, the Messiah connects those who believed and followed God's plan under Noah and were lifted up safely in the ark to those who follow God's plan through the Messiah (which includes becoming the spiritual bride) being taken up to safety (verses 40–42). For a fuller explanation of the Lord's teaching in Matthew, see pages 250–252 in *The Messianic Feast*.

8

The Excellent Benefits of the Holy Spirit Infilling

This chapter will first clarify that the Messiah's baptism and the Holy Spirit infilling are often two separate phases. From there, we will go on to focus on being filled with the Holy Spirit and consider the excellent benefits of this gift.

8.1   THE MESSIAH'S HOLY SPIRIT BAPTISM AND THE HOLY SPIRIT INFILLING

To properly understand the Holy Spirit baptism that Jesus was called to usher in (also called "the baptism in the Holy Spirit" or "the Messiah's Baptism"), it is important to see that the "infilling" of the Spirit is often a second step. While it is commonly taught that the baptism in the Holy Spirit is the same thing as when a person becomes Spirit-filled, that view does not harmonize with all of the scriptures, as we will see.

The Holy Spirit baptism that Jesus was to bring is directly contrasted to John's baptism in water several times in the scriptures (Matthew 3:11; Mark 1:8; Luke 3:16; John 1:33; Acts 1:5; and Acts 11:16). John's baptism was a ritual washing that pointed forward to the true spiritual washing, which is the Messiah's Holy Spirit baptism. This Holy Spirit baptism that Jesus provides takes place when one believes in his sacrifice on the cross and receives his cleansing and forgiveness. When we repent and ask Jesus to forgive us and come into our hearts, we are "born again" (born from above) by God's Spirit.

Jesus explains this born-again experience in John 3 (see chapter 9, section 3 for more on this), where he essentially says that this second "birth" is needed to see the kingdom of God (i.e., attain salvation). He states that one needs to be born (generated) from above by the Spirit of

God. This is the Messiah's baptism that provides the cleansing and forgiveness necessary for one to be ready to commune with God and enter into His presence. Thus, his Holy Spirit baptism/washing is required for salvation, but the Holy Spirit infilling is a second phase—and not required for salvation.

We see these two steps in various scriptures. Below, the apostles in Jerusalem understand that there are Samaritans wheo believed, received Jesus, and were baptized (either in water or washed by believing—i.e., the Messiah's baptism), but they had not yet received the Holy Spirit:

> ^{NAS} Acts 8:14–17 Now when the apostles in Jerusalem heard that Samaria **had received the word of God**, they sent them Peter and John, who came down and prayed for them, **that they might receive the Holy Spirit**. For He had not yet fallen upon any of them; they had simply been **baptized in the name of the Lord Jesus**. Then they *began* laying their hands on them, and they were receiving the Holy Spirit.

Later, in the Book of Acts, we see that Paul also understood that not all believers are filled with the Holy Spirit. In Acts 19:2, he comes across some disciples who he thinks are believers in Christ, and he asks if they received the Holy Spirit **when** they believed:

> ^{NAS} Acts 19:1–2b And it came about that while Apollos was at Corinth, Paul having passed through the upper country came to Ephesus, and found some disciples, ² and he said to them, "Did you receive the Holy Spirit **when you believed?**"

Therefore, Paul definitely understands that every believer does not immediately receive the Holy Spirit *infilling* when they believe. After Paul realizes that these were disciples of John the Baptist and not yet of Jesus, he explains the good news of the Messiah to them. They then receive the Lord Jesus and are baptized/washed either by water or spiritually washed by believing:

> NAS Acts 19:4-6 And Paul said, "John baptized with the baptism of repentance, telling the people to believe in Him who was coming after him, that is, in Jesus." And when they heard this, they were baptized in the name of the Lord Jesus.

Whether this was water baptism after believing or becoming spiritually washed when they believed, the point is they are now believers. Paul then moves to the second phase—that they might receive the infilling of the Holy Spirit:

> NAS Acts 19:6 And **when** Paul had laid his hands upon them, the Holy Spirit came on them, and they *began* speaking with tongues and prophesying.

These examples prove that the Holy Spirit baptism/washing that Jesus would bring in (believing and being washed) is not the same as the *infilling* of the Holy Spirit (i.e., being Spirit-filled).

Peter tells the Jews, who were witnessing the events on the day of Pentecost, that if they repent and be baptized/washed "in the name of Jesus Christ" for forgiveness of sins, that they *shall* (future tense) receive the gift of the Holy Spirit.

> NAS Acts 2:38 And Peter *said* to them, "Repent, and let each of you **be baptized** in the name of Jesus Christ **for the forgiveness of your sins**; and you shall receive the gift of the Holy Spirit.

After they are baptized/washed by believing in Jesus, they are then in a place where they are ready to "receive the gift of the Holy Spirit."

It is true that some receive the infilling of the Holy Spirit at the same time they believe, like the newly believing Gentiles later in the book of Acts, just as Peter was preaching Christ to them:

> NAS Acts 10:44-47 While Peter was still speaking these words, the **Holy Spirit fell upon all those who were lis-**

> tening to the message. ⁴⁵ And all the circumcised believers who had come with Peter were amazed, because the gift of the Holy Spirit had been poured out upon the Gentiles also. ⁴⁶ **For they were hearing them speaking with tongues** and exalting God. Then Peter answered, ⁴⁷ "Surely no one can refuse the water for these to be baptized who have **received the Holy Spirit just as we** *did*, can he?"

Yet, many do not receive the Holy Spirit infilling until sometime after they believe (Acts 1:5; 2:4, 33; 8:14–17; 9:17; 19:6), and these examples make it clear there are two phases involved. The infilling of the Holy Spirit comes with an ability to pray in the spirit (called speaking in tongues, Acts 2:3–11; 8:18–20; 10:45–46; 19:6; Romans 8:26–27; 1 Corinthians 14:14–19, 39).

The Holy Spirit baptism of the original apostles (Acts 2) was somewhat of a unique case. Although they, of course, were believers in Jesus before his death and resurrection, the Messiah's baptism (being born from above) could not take place until after his atoning sacrifice (John 7:37–39; 16:7). Then, several days before Pentecost, Jesus told them that this promised baptism (per John 1:33; Matthew 3:11; Mark 1:8; Luke 3:16) was about to begin:

> ᴺᴬˢ Acts 1:5 for John baptized with water, **but you shall be baptized** with the Holy Spirit **not many days from now.**"

Thus, when comparing that scripture to the one below, it is clear that the apostles, like the Gentiles later, were baptized/washed with the Holy Spirit (the Messiah's baptism) and filled with the Holy Spirit at the very same time:

> ᴺᴬˢ Acts 2:4 And they were all filled with the Holy Spirit and began to speak with other tongues, as the Spirit was giving them utterance.

The Holy Spirit baptism (washing) with the infilling that sometimes followed was the fulfillment of the promise of the father that God had spoken to the Jewish prophets Isaiah, Ezekiel, and Joel (Isaiah 28:11-12; Ezekiel 36:26-27; Joel 2:28). This is what Jesus explained was about to begin (Luke 24:49; Acts 1:4), and Peter shows this was confirmed at Pentecost (Acts 2:33).

8.2 THE HOLY SPIRIT QUENCHES OUR SPIRITUAL THIRST

On the last day of the Feast of Tabernacles, Jesus cried out in the Temple concerning the outpouring of God's Spirit, which he would soon be ushering in:

> NAS John 7:37-40 Now on the last day, the great *day* of the feast, Jesus stood and cried out, saying, "If any man is thirsty, let him come to Me and drink. "He who believes in Me, as the Scripture said, 'From his innermost being shall flow rivers of living water.'" **But this He spoke of the Spirit**, whom **those who believed in Him were to receive**; for the Spirit was not yet *given*, because Jesus was not yet glorified. *Some* of the multitude therefore, when they heard these words, were saying, "This certainly is the Prophet."

To have rivers of living water (spiritually speaking) coming from our innermost being is, of course, a huge benefit of receiving the Holy Spirit. This completely satisfies our spiritual thirst, and this scripture says that Jesus was speaking of the Spirit here, and that those who believe in the Messiah were to receive this blessing. This also enables the believer to have living waters (spiritually) to pour forth to others from their innermost being.

Jesus said essentially the same things to the Samaritan woman at Jacob's well, adding that those who drink the water that he will give would no longer thirst, again speaking spiritually of partaking of God's Spirit:

> NAS John 4:7-14 There came a woman of Samaria to draw water. Jesus said to her, "Give Me a drink." For His disciples

had gone away into the city to buy food. The Samaritan woman therefore said to Him, "How is it that You, being a Jew, ask me for a drink since I am a Samaritan woman?" (For Jews have no dealings with Samaritans.) Jesus answered and said to her, "**If you knew the gift of God**, and who it is who says to you, 'Give Me a drink,' you would have asked Him, and He would have **given you living water**." She said to Him, "Sir, You have nothing to draw with and the well is deep; where then do You get that living water? "You are not greater than our father Jacob, are You, who gave us the well, and drank of it himself, and his sons, and his cattle?" Jesus answered and said to her, "Everyone who drinks of this water shall thirst again; but **whoever drinks of the water that I shall give him shall never thirst**; but **the water that I shall give him shall become in him a well of water springing up to eternal life.**"

8.3 THE HOLY SPIRIT BRINGS JOY, COMFORT, AND REST

The Holy Spirit brings joy:

> NAS Romans 14:17 for the kingdom of God is not eating and drinking, but righteousness and peace and **joy in the Holy Spirit**.

> NAS Romans 15:13 Now may the God of hope fill you with all joy and peace in believing, that you may abound in hope by the power of the Holy Spirit.

> NAS 1 Thessalonians 1:6 You also became imitators of us and of the Lord, having received the word in much tribulation with the joy of the Holy Spirit,

Receiving the infilling of God's Spirit brings comfort:

> ^{NAS} Acts 9:31 So the church throughout all Judea and Galilee and Samaria enjoyed peace, being built up; and, going on in the fear of the Lord **and in the comfort of the Holy Spirit, it continued to increase.**

> ^{KJV} John 14:16 And I will pray the Father, and **he shall give you another Comforter, that he may abide with you for ever**;

We will see a little later that Paul connects the verse below from Isaiah to receiving the Holy Spirit, where God promised that it would bring rest to the weary soul:

> ^{NAS} Isaiah 28:11–12 Indeed, He will speak to this people Through **stammering lips and a foreign tongue**, He who said to them, "**Here is rest, give rest to the weary**," And, "**Here is repose**," but they would not listen.

> ^{KJV} Matthew 11:28–30 Come unto me, all *ye* that labour and are heavy laden, **and I will give you rest**. Take my yoke upon you, and learn of me; for I am meek and lowly in heart: and ye shall find rest unto your souls. For my yoke *is* easy, and my burden is light.

8.4 GOD'S HOLY SPIRIT WILL LEAD AND TEACH US

Receiving the Holy Spirit enables one to be more sensitive to spiritual truth:

> ^{NAS} John 14:26 "**But the Helper, the Holy Spirit**, whom the Father will send in My name, **He will teach you all things, and bring to your remembrance all that I said to you.**

The Holy Spirit within helps teach us to discern spiritual things. Notice that the natural man, without the spirit, cannot receive the same spiritual discernment:

> ^{YLT} 1 Corinthians 2:13–14   which things also we speak, **not in words taught by human wisdom, but in those taught by the Holy Spirit, with spiritual things spiritual things comparing,** and the natural man doth not receive the things of the Spirit of God, for to him they are foolishness, and he is not able to know *them*, because spiritually they are discerned;

The Holy Spirit teaches by way of typology, showing what certain events and items in the Old Covenant represented and pointed forward to:

> ^{NIV} Hebrews 9:7   But only the high priest entered the inner room, and that only once a year, and never without blood, which he offered for himself and for the sins the people had committed in ignorance.

> ^{DBY} Hebrews 9:8   **the Holy Spirit shewing this**, that the way of the *holy of* holies has not yet been made manifest while as yet the first tabernacle has *its* standing;

The Messiah's baptism makes a way for every believer to now enter the holiest place where God's presence dwells. This could not have been done while the Old Covenant still had legal standing, as verse 8 above states.

The Holy Spirit will bear witness to the things Jesus said and to who he was:

> ^{KJV} John 15:26   But when the Comforter is come, whom I will send unto you from the Father, *even* the Spirit of truth, which proceedeth from the Father, **he shall testify of me**:

Receiving the infilling of God's Spirit will help guide us into all truth and will also help us discern things that are to come:

> ^{NAS} John 16:13   "But when He, the Spirit of truth, comes, **He will guide you into all the truth**; for He will not speak on His own initiative, but whatever He hears, He will speak; and

8. The Excellent Benefits of the Holy Spirit Infilling

He will disclose to you what is to come.

Teachers who are led by the Holy Spirit will know to not lay heavy burdens (such as guilt and condemnation) upon the flock:

> NAS Acts 15:28–29 "For **it seemed good to the Holy Spirit and to us to lay upon you no greater burden** than these essentials: that you abstain from things sacrificed to idols and from blood and from things strangled and from fornication; if you keep yourselves free from such things, you will do well. Farewell."

The Holy Spirit also gives power:

> NAS Acts 1:8 **but you shall receive power when the Holy Spirit has come upon you**; and you shall be My witnesses both in Jerusalem, and in all Judea and Samaria, and even to the remotest part of the earth."

> NAS Luke 24:49 "And behold, I am sending forth the promise of My Father upon you; but you are to stay in the city until you are **clothed with power from on high**."

8.5 SPEAKING IN TONGUES IS THE SIGN OF RECEIVING

Time and time again in the scriptures, we see that speaking in tongues is the sign of receiving the Holy Spirit. This is the outward sign of receiving the Holy Spirit:

> NAS Acts 2:4 And they were all filled with the Holy Spirit **and began to speak with other tongues, as the Spirit was giving them utterance.**

> NAS Acts 2:33 "Therefore having been exalted to the right hand of God, and having received **from the Father the**

promise of the Holy Spirit, He has poured forth this which you both **see and hear.**

When Philip went to Samaria, many came to believe in the Lord through his preaching:

> ^{NAS} Acts 8:12 But when they believed Philip preaching the good news about the kingdom of God and the name of Jesus Christ, they were being baptized, men and women alike.

So these Samaritans believed and were baptized (possibly meaning washed spiritually in their manner of speaking—the Messiah's Spirit baptism), yet they had not received the Holy Spirit infilling. And when the apostles heard that these new believers had not yet received the Holy Spirit, they sent Peter and John to them:

> ^{NAS} Acts 8:14-17 Now when the apostles in Jerusalem heard that Samaria had received the word of God, they sent them Peter and John, who came down and prayed for them, **that they might receive the Holy Spirit. For He had not yet fallen upon any of them**; they had **simply been baptized in the name of the Lord Jesus**. Then they *began* laying their hands on them, **and they were receiving the Holy Spirit**.

Again, it's very possible that when this verse says the Samaritans were "baptized," it uses the first-century Jewish idiom where it means they were spiritually washed by believing in the Lord Jesus (more on this event in chapter 9, section 7). But it's also possible that Philip had these Samaritans water baptized, not yet fully understanding New Covenant truth.

Either way, the point is that although the verse below does not specifically say they spoke in tongues, it does say that Simon **saw** that they received the Holy Spirit when the apostles prayed for them; seeing them speaking in tongues (just as Acts 2:33) is most likely what he saw:

> ^{NAS} Acts 8:18-19 Now when Simon **saw that the Spirit was bestowed** through the laying on of the apostles' hands, he offered them money, saying, "Give this authority to me as well, so that everyone on whom I lay my hands **may receive the Holy Spirit**."

And then Peter rebuked him for thinking the gift of God (also called the gift of the Holy Spirit, Acts 2:38; 10:45; Hebrews 6:4) could be purchased with money:

> ^{NAS} Acts 8:20 But Peter said to him, "May your silver perish with you, because you thought you could obtain the **gift of God** with money!

And in Acts, chapter 10, how did Jewish Messianic believers know that the Gentiles were filled with the Holy Spirit? Because (for) they were hearing them speak in tongues:

> ^{NAS} Acts 10:45 And all the circumcised believers who had come with Peter **were amazed, because the gift of the Holy Spirit had been poured out** upon the Gentiles also. **For they were hearing them speaking with tongues** and exalting God. Then Peter answered,

The disciples in Acts 19 were baptized/washed by believing in Jesus (Acts 19:4-5). Then Paul prays that they receive the Holy Spirit, and they begin speaking in tongues when they are filled:

> ^{NAS} Acts 19:6 And when Paul had laid his hands upon them, **the Holy Spirit came on them, and they** *began* **speaking with tongues** and prophesying.

8.6   WHY SPEAK IN TONGUES?

Now that we have discussed receiving the Holy Spirit, let us examine more benefits of this gift.

For anyone who is unsure what speaking in tongues means, it is a heavenly prayer language in which a Spirit-filled believer can pray directly to God. In rare instances (such as in Acts 2:4–12), God may inspire one to speak in a known earthly language that is not their own, but normally, speaking in tongues is in an unknown language. The human spirit speaks directly to God and bypasses the natural mind:

> NAS 1 Corinthians 14:2   For one who speaks in a tongue does not speak to men, but to God; for no one understands, but in *his* spirit he speaks mysteries.

> NAS 1 Corinthians 14:14   For if I pray in a tongue, **my spirit prays**, but my mind is unfruitful.

> NAS Jude 1:20   But you, beloved, building yourselves up on your most holy faith; praying in the Holy Spirit;

Praying in tongues builds up (edifies) one's own spirit:

> NAS 1 Corinthians 14:4   **One who speaks in a tongue edifies himself**; but one who prophesies edifies the church.

In the context of the verse above, Paul qualifies that, if people speak in tongues the entire time when they gather together for fellowship, their own spirit will be edified but not those of others who are hearing, especially any who are not yet believers. In this section of scripture, Paul thanks God that he speaks in tongues more than anyone else, but he gives the qualification that when people gather together, they should allow some praying in tongues but that using the known language is better for most of the public service (1 Corinthians 14:5, 18–19, 39). Here is some of what Paul wrote:

> NAS 1 Corinthians 14:14-19 For if I pray in a tongue, my spirit prays, but my mind is unfruitful. What is *the outcome* then? I shall pray with the spirit and I shall pray with the mind also; I shall sing with the spirit and I shall sing with the mind also. Otherwise if you bless in the spirit *only*, how will the one who fills the place of the ungifted say the "Amen" at your giving of thanks, since he does not know what you are saying? For you are giving thanks well enough, but the other man is not edified. I thank God, I speak in tongues more than you all; however, in the church I desire to speak five words with my mind, that I may instruct others also, rather than ten thousand words in a tongue.

Paul shows that speaking in tongues was a promised sign spoken of in the Old Testament, and he applies this verse to how God was moving in Paul's day:

> NAS 1 Corinthians 14:21-22 In the Law it is written, "**By men of strange tongues** and by the lips of strangers **I will speak to this people**, and even so they will not listen to Me," says the Lord. So then tongues are for a sign, not to those who believe, but to unbelievers; but prophecy *is for a sign*, not to unbelievers, but to those who believe.

This speaking in tongues and bringing **spiritual rest** to the weary had been prophesied in Isaiah:

> NAS Isaiah 28:11-12 Indeed, He will speak to this people Through stammering lips and a foreign tongue, He who said to them, "**Here is rest, give rest to the weary**," And, "Here is repose," but they would not listen.

8.7 THE HOLY SPIRIT IS NEEDED TO PREPARE THE SPIRITUAL BRIDE

The scriptures relate a major event that is yet to be fulfilled—a group of believers who prepare and make themselves ready as the (spiritual) bride of the Messiah:

> NAS Revelation 19:7 "Let us rejoice and be glad and give the glory to Him, for the marriage of the Lamb has come and **His bride has made herself ready.**"

One way for us to become prepared as this bride is to purify ourselves even as he is pure:

> NIV 1 John 3:2–3 Dear friends, now we are children of God, and what we will be has not yet been made known. But we know that when he appears, we shall be like him, for we shall see him as he is. **Everyone who has this hope in him purifies himself**, just as he is pure.

This chapter began by quoting Jesus explaining that the gift of God would be like rivers of living water coming **out from** the believer (speaking of the Spirit of God, John 7:37–40; John 4:7–14). This spiritual flow from God to one another may be the most important part of the spiritual bride making herself ready, the spiritual sustenance and supply coming **to and from** each member in the spiritual body:

> NAS Ephesians 4:15–16 but speaking the truth in love, we are to grow up in all *aspects* into Him, who is the head, *even* Christ, from whom the whole body, being fitted and held together **by that which every joint supplies**, according to the proper working of **each individual part, causes the growth of the body** for **the building up of itself in love.**

Receiving this gift of God is not difficult; the Holy Spirit comes by prayer, as the believer asks God for it:

> ^{NIV} Luke 11:13 If you then, though you are evil, [50] know how to give good gifts to your children, how much more will your Father in heaven give the Holy Spirit to those who ask him!"

It is important to remember that all of these blessings and benefits of receiving the Holy Spirit are not one-time events. The rest and refreshing that the Spirit brings can be experienced whenever one steps into it. This gift is for any time one is in need. When Jude, verse 20 speaks of "building yourselves up on your most holy faith; praying in the Holy Spirit," this is something we can enter into at any time of day, whenever one desires.

---

50   One of the definitions UBS gives for this Greek word is "sinful." Most translations use "evil" or "wicked" here, and I don't think that is what the Lord is saying to his disciples—that they are wicked and evil. I believe "sinful" more closely reflects what the Lord means here.

9

Some Additional Baptism Scriptures Explained

In this chapter, I will cover a number of baptism events and scriptures that have not yet been mentioned or fully covered elsewhere in this book. As we go through these various scriptures, I will refer to the following list of twelve reasons that dispute water baptism. To avoid the repetition of writing out every reason in this list after each particular baptism event covered here, I list the numbered reasons that apply to that specific baptism verse, and the reader can then refer back to this list.

For instance, when I discuss the scriptures in section 9.12, titled "Acts 19:1–7: The Baptism/Washing in Ephesus," I write "See reasons 1–12" because all twelve reasons from the list below apply there.

9.1 LIST OF TWELVE REASONS AGAINST WATER BAPTISM IN THE NEW COVENANT

1. It may seem surprising, but there is not one single scripture where Jesus ever specifically said anyone should **water** baptize. If water baptism is necessary for salvation and if it's what the Messiah wanted for the New Covenant, shouldn't he have recommended it just one time in scripture? And shouldn't Jesus have made the correct formula clear to us if he truly wanted water baptism?

2. Since Jesus was focused on the promised Holy Spirit baptism and infilling that he would bring in, wouldn't it make more sense that when he told the disciples to go out baptizing the nations that he meant to bring the Spirit baptism and not the Old Covenant water baptism that God told John to bring in? There are times he mentions

baptism (some are clearly spiritual/figurative, such as Matthew 20:22, 23), but in other scriptures, like Matthew 28:19, commentators from the time of Rome have mistakenly assumed he meant **water** baptism. However, it makes much more sense that he was speaking of the Spirit baptism/washing that God, John the Baptist, and Peter all said the Messiah would bring (Matthew 3:11; Mark 1:8; Luke 3:16; John 1:33; Acts 1:5; 11:16).

3. Why is it that every time Jesus speaks of the baptisms (John with water, **but** Jesus with the Holy Spirit), he contrasts the two? He never joins them together as if both would be needed, but instead he always **contrasts** them by using the word "but."

> NAS Acts 11:16 "And I remembered the word of the Lord, **how He used to say,** 'John baptized **with water, but** you shall be **baptized with the Holy Spirit.**'

See also Acts 1:5.

4. The same is true with John the Baptist—he always **contrasts** his water baptism to the Holy Spirit baptism that the Messiah would bring, and he never once joins them as if both would continue together. While still in the Old Covenant, John the Baptist says that God called **him** to baptize **in water**, but that the Messiah would baptize in **the Holy Spirit**:

> NAS John 1:33 "And I did not recognize Him, but **He who sent me** to baptize **in water** said to me, 'He upon whom you see the Spirit descending and remaining upon Him, **this is the one who baptizes in the Holy Spirit.**'

See also Matthew 3:11; Mark 1:8; and Luke 3:16, where John contrasts the two baptisms every time. John was called by God to baptize in water, but the Messiah never was.

5. The Greek word "*baptizo*" (baptize) in the first-century idiom had a primary meaning of "wash, washed, washing, and immersed," which is different than the English ritualistic meaning that occurs when most Christians think of baptism, which itself has been handed down to us through Rome. This is important for interpreting certain scriptures. When we see the word "baptize," we mostly think immediately of the Christian rite of water baptism, whereas to these early Jews, it referred to being washed or ritually washed, often in a spiritual sense. (See chapters 2, 3, and 5 for this history.)

6. The natural-to-spiritual idiom of the Jews must also be understood, for they would often speak the natural word but mean the spiritual truth behind it (see chapter 4). When we see the Greek word for baptize used in the New Covenant period, are we sure that they are going backward to the literal *water* baptism, or is the verse speaking of the Messiah's Spirit baptism? Is the verse talking about an Old Covenant water baptism, or is it speaking of the washing (baptism) that comes when one believes in Jesus (the same washing the Jews were accustomed to but in a New Covenant spiritual sense—that of being spiritually washed by accepting the forgiveness the Messiah established)?

7. Paul, during the New Testament period, says Christ did not send him to baptize (1 Corinthians 1:17). If water baptism was an important command that was to continue alongside the Messiah's Spirit baptism in the New Covenant, Paul would not say such a thing.

8. Paul thanks God that he baptized only a few people, because he understands that it is no longer God's will in the New Covenant (1 Corinthians 1:14). Paul would **not** thank God that he baptized only a few people if water baptism were an important command for the New Covenant (whether accused of reciting the formula wrong in his own name or not). Instead, Paul would follow God's commands, without fear of what men might say.

9. In Hebrews, chapter 9, Paul makes it clear when he uses the Greek word for baptism and says that the various water baptisms/washings are no longer imposed in the New Covenant:

> NIV Hebrews 9:9–10 This is an illustration for the present time, indicating that the gifts and sacrifices being offered were not able to clear the conscience of the worshiper. They are only a matter of food and drink and **various ceremonial washings—external regulations** applying **until** the time of the new order.

Note that the Greek word translated as "ceremonial washings" by this translation is *baptismos* (baptisms).

10. If water baptism were really to continue alongside the Messiah's Spirit baptism in the New Covenant, why does Paul say there is one baptism (Ephesians 4:5)? And the one baptism that continues is **not water** baptism; it is the Spirit baptism/washing that Jesus provided:

> NAS 1 Corinthians 12:13 For **by one Spirit we were all baptized** into one body, whether Jews or Greeks, whether slaves or free, and we were all made to drink of one Spirit.

11. In the New Covenant, Jesus is concerned with getting Paul filled with the Holy Spirit, not with getting him water baptized (Acts 9:17), and that was also Paul's focus (Acts 19:2). The same focus on the Holy Spirit infilling is true for the other apostles (Acts 8:14–17).

12. From a New Covenant perspective, after seeing all of the evidence provided, is a ritual immersion in water using a certain formula what the Messiah really wanted? After repenting and asking forgiveness from God, believing in the Messiah, and appropriating the shed blood of Christ for remission of sins, does a baptism in water still need to be performed to be cleansed and right with God? Having received the Messiah's promised Spirit baptism/washing and then filled with God's Holy Spirit (the promise of the Father), does one still need to be water baptized to remove one's sins?

Chapters 2 and 5 in this book have revealed that in the Jewish idiom, the words "wash" and "baptize" were almost interchangeable. Tradition from Rome has essentially taught us to put on water baptism glasses, so to speak, so that we picture a water ritual every time we see the word "baptism," whereas in the Jewish Messianic idiom, it often meant *spiritually* washed instead.

With these twelve reasons summarized, let us now examine these baptism events and scriptures.

9.2 MATTHEW 3:13-17: WHY WAS JESUS WATER BAPTIZED?

(See reason 9.)

John the Baptist's water baptism was said to be a baptism of repentance (Matthew 3:11; Acts 19:4) in that it was to prepare the people so that the Messiah might be revealed to Israel:

> ^{NIV} John 1:31 I myself did not know him, but the reason I came baptizing with water was **that he might be revealed to Israel**."

When the Messiah came to John for water baptism, John knew by the spirit that something was wrong with his baptizing the Messiah for repentance, and John tried to prevent him:

> ^{NAS} Matthew 3:14 But John **tried to prevent Him**, saying, "**I have need to be baptized by You**, and do You come to me?"

> ^{NAS} Matthew 3:15 But Jesus answering said to him, "Permit *it* at this time; for in this way it is fitting for us to **fulfill all righteousness**." Then he permitted Him.

Why would the Messiah, who was sinless and had nothing to repent for, be water baptized by John?

Remember, the scripture says that Jesus was a man (1 Timothy 2:5), and he was then under the Old Covenant law at this time; some of the ritual washings in water were part of the instructions from God, including John the Baptist's. So, as a man, Jesus was fully under these laws. These water baptisms (those commanded by God) were also for ritual cleansing after coming in contact with any unclean person or thing.

Although John's baptism focused on repentance, it was also a ritual washing to prepare for a special visitation from God (John 1:31). And, when John baptized the Messiah, a visitation from God did indeed take place:

> ^{NAS} Matthew 3:16–17 And after being baptized, Jesus went up immediately from the water; **and behold, the heavens were opened**, and he saw **the Spirit of God descending** as a dove, *and* **coming upon Him**, and behold, **a voice out of the heavens**, saying, "**This is My beloved Son, in whom I am well-pleased**."

Remember that John had at first tried to talk the Messiah out of it, saying, "I need to be baptized by you," but the Messiah's words that he must "fulfill all righteousness" caused John to understand.

UBS Lexicon defines this Greek word translated as "righteousness" in John 1:31 above as "What God requires,"[51] and *Thayer's Greek Lexicon* says "the condition acceptable to God."[52] Since Jesus was a man under God's law, he aligned with "what God requires" by staying consistent with this Old Covenant water baptism that would bring about "the condition acceptable to God." God then demonstrated His acceptance by opening the heavens and His spirit then descended on Jesus as soon as he came up out of the water.

Since the Messiah's baptism was not yet available, the water baptism God sent John to bring was a symbolic act that pointed forward and stood in until the true Spirit baptism came in:

> NAS John 1:33 "And I did not recognize Him, but **He who sent me to baptize in water** said to me, 'He upon whom you see the Spirit descending and remaining upon Him, **this is the one who baptizes in the Holy Spirit.**'
>
> NIV Hebrews 9:10 They are only a matter of food and drink and various **ceremonial washings**—external regulations **applying until** the time of the new order.

9.3 JOHN 3: BORN AGAIN, AND THE SUPPOSED BAPTISMAL REGENERATION

(See reason 1.)

I cover this portion of scripture, not because it has anything to do with water baptism, but only because certain individuals like Tertullian have attached it to water baptism, saying it proves it is necessary for salvation. This scripture occurs when Nicodemus, a high-ranking member

---

51   *UBS Greek-English Dictionary*, p. 46.
52   *The New Thayer's Greek-English Lexicon of the New Testament*, p. 149.

9. SOME ADDITIONAL BAPTISM SCRIPTURES EXPLAINED 119

of the Jewish Sanhedrin, comes to Jesus secretly by night with some questions. Remember that the Greek words translated as "born again" can also mean "born from above":

> NAS John 3:1–5 Now there was a man of the Pharisees, named Nicodemus, a ruler of the Jews; this man came to Him by night, and said to Him, "Rabbi, we know that You have come from God *as* a teacher; for no one can do these signs that You do unless God is with him." Jesus answered and said to him, "Truly, truly, I say to you, unless one is **born again**, he cannot see the kingdom of God." Nicodemus said to Him, "How can a man be born when he is old? **He cannot enter a second time into his mother's womb** and be born, can he?" Jesus answered, "Truly, truly, I say to you, unless one is born of water **and the Spirit**, he cannot enter into the kingdom of God.

The Messiah obviously refers to what Nicodemus said about the mother's womb (the first "birth"), saying that more than this is needed to see the kingdom of God—that is, being born (generated) from above by the Spirit of God. Nicodemus was a scholar among the Jews. And as a side note, his question was obviously not a serious one (a man going into his mother a second time to be born again), but asking such a question was a common Jewish method of seeking another clue to the parable that Jesus spoke.

Tertullian speaks of this portion of scripture when he lays down the prescript that Jesus here refers to water baptism:

> "without baptism, salvation is attainable by none," (chiefly on the ground of that declaration of the Lord, who says, "Unless one be born of water, he hath not life"),...[53]

This concept from Rome gave birth to the doctrine called "baptismal regeneration," where one is birthed, cleansed from sin, saved, and re-

---

53 Roberts and Donaldson, *Ante-Nicene Fathers*, vol. 3, pp. 674–675.

generated in the waters of baptism. However, Jesus does not mention baptism anywhere in this discussion. In fact, he is saying that one can see the kingdom of God only when "born again" ("born from above") **by the spirit**. And one is clearly born from above after accepting the Messiah and getting cleansed from sin, not after being baptized in water.

God proves this in Acts 10:44–48, where the Gentiles believe in the word of God, are washed from their sins, and then God fills them with the Holy Spirit—all while they had not been **water** baptized. We know that God does not fill unclean, unsaved sinners with His Holy Spirit.

Jesus makes his words on being born "again" (or, from above) clear in this context, where he explains that the one born of water (through the water sac in their mothers' womb) is flesh, and would still need to be regenerated from above by God's Spirit:

> NAS John 3:6–8 "That which is **born of the flesh** is flesh, and that which is **born of the Spirit** is spirit. "Do not marvel that I said to you, 'You must be born again.' "The wind blows where it wishes and you hear the sound of it, but do not know where it comes from and where it is going; so is **everyone who is born of the Spirit**."

Without being regenerated from above by accepting the Messiah, our spirit cannot directly access God (John 14:6; Romans 8:10; Hebrews 10:19). The Messiah was showing the need to be born from above by being "born of the spirit" (verse 8). He was not teaching what became known in Rome as baptismal regeneration through a water baptism rite.

Just a few verses later, the Lord makes this clear in his conversation with Nicodemus—that salvation and cleansing (born again) come by believing:

> NAS John 3:15 that **whoever believes** may in Him have eternal life.

^{NAS}John 3:16 "For God so loved the world, that He gave His only begotten Son, that **whoever believes** in Him should not perish, but have eternal life.

There is nothing here about water baptism saving anyone—it's believing in the Messiah and thereby receiving the spirit washing. This is the Messiah's baptism, where the believer is washed/baptized and is then ready to receive the Holy Spirit infilling (Acts 2:4; 8:14–17; 9:17; 19:6).

^{NIV}Titus 3:5 he saved us, not because of righteous things we had done, but because of his mercy. He **saved us** through the **washing of rebirth** and renewal **by the Holy Spirit**,

9.4 JOHN 3:22-23 AND JOHN 4:1: THE DISCIPLES OF CHRIST WATER BAPTIZING

(See reason 1.)

Although his disciples water baptized (John 3:22–23, 26), the scripture specifically states that Jesus himself was not water baptizing (John 4:1–2). This again was during the Old Testament period when the Messiah's baptism was not yet available. But if God called Jesus to water baptize, then why is he not joining the disciples in this?

Jesus did not do the various traditional religious requirements of his day when God was not leading him to. He did not ritually wash (the Greek says "baptize himself") before the meal with the Pharisee (Luke 11:38), and his disciples did not wash their hands before eating bread (Matthew 15:2).

And if we say that Christ's office was higher than for him to water baptize anyone and thus he appointed his disciples to do it instead, then that would be contrary to his own teaching. After all, he was humble enough to wash his disciples' feet (John 13:5–14), so he certainly did not walk this earth too exalted to personally water baptize believers, if God had actually called him to it. However, God never called Jesus to water baptize, but rather to bring forth the Holy Spirit baptism (Matthew 3:11; Mark 1:8; Luke 3:16; John 1:33; Acts 1:5; 11:16).

9.5 WATER BAPTISMS IN THE BOOK OF ACTS: A TIME OF TRANSITION

(See reasons 1–12.)

There is no question that the apostles did not understand all spiritual truth after the resurrection and early on in the New Covenant. This may sound heretical to some, but please consider the following scriptures. Just the night before his crucifixion, Jesus told the apostles that they were still not ready for all of the truth he wanted to teach them:

> NAS John 16:12 "I have many more things to say to you, but you cannot bear *them* now.

Then, on the day of the resurrection, they prove they did not have a complete understanding because they refused to believe Mary Magdalene and the other women who said that Jesus had risen from the dead (just as he had promised) and that they had seen him. Jesus strongly reproves them for this:

> NAS Mark 16:14 And afterward He appeared to the eleven themselves as they were reclining *at the table*; and **He reproached them for their unbelief and hardness of heart**, because they had not believed those who had seen Him after He had risen.

Then, way down in Acts, chapter 10, we see that Peter is still refusing to eat with Gentiles and is seeing all Gentiles as unclean, until God reveals this New Covenant truth to him:

> NAS Acts 10:28b and *yet* **God has shown me** that I should not call **any man** unholy or unclean.

So there is no question that the apostles were coming into new truth as they went along. Some of the water baptism events in Acts are therefore part of this transition period, especially when we consider the scriptures contrary to water baptism from Paul. Keep in mind that they were still meeting regularly in the Temple (Acts 2:46; 5:42), where immersion in water (baptism) was a requirement before entering (as covered in chapter 2).

Out of all of the apostles, Paul was the most advanced at moving into a better understanding of the New Covenant. The scriptures show that he was also the best Bible scholar with the most revelations (2 Corinthians 12:7; Galatians 2:11; 2 Peter 3:15). Paul was educated in the scriptures under Gamaliel, apparently from a young age (Acts 22:3).

We have also seen that, early on in his ministry, Paul spent eighteen months in Corinth, where he founded and built up the Corinthian Church (Acts 18:7–11). During those eighteen months, he baptized only a handful of believers because he understood the truth on water baptisms very early on. He wrote to the Corinthians, later saying that "Christ did not send me to baptize." He also wrote to the fellowship in Ephesus and declared that there is only **one** baptism, **not** two important baptisms (Ephesians 4:5).

In his very first letter to the Corinthians (after saying that Christ did not send him to baptize), he tells them what the **one** remaining baptism is and that it is the Messiah's Spirit baptism:

> NAS 1 Corinthians 12:13 For **by one Spirit we were all baptized** into one body, whether Jews or Greeks, whether slaves or free, and we were all made to drink of one Spirit.

Paul is teaching the Messiah's promised Spirit baptism here, not a water one. Yet, we see other times where Paul does fulfill certain Old Covenant requirements for the sake of the ministry, to not stumble others, or for various other reasons. He wrote that he became as a Jew that he might win them (1 Corinthians 9:20). Thus, he sometimes went along with certain religious norms so that he could continue to minister to certain groups. One example of this is where Paul follows certain requirements of the law, such as giving notice of his ritual purification to enter the Temple with the appropriate animal sacrifices offered:

> ^{NAS} Acts 21:26 Then Paul took the men, and the next day, purifying himself along with them, went into the temple, giving notice of the completion of the days of purification, until the sacrifice was offered for each one of them.

Another example in the Book of Acts is where Paul has Timothy circumcised, even though Paul actually taught against circumcision (Acts 21:21; 1 Corinthians 7:18-19; Galatians 5:2-4). He had Timothy circumcised so they could freely minister to certain Jewish groups who would otherwise have been concerned with ritual purity:

> ^{NAS} Acts 16:3 Paul wanted this man to go with him; and he took him and circumcised him because of the Jews who were in those parts, for they all knew that his father was a Greek.

So there were various times when requirements of the ceremonial law were adhered to so as to freely enter the Temple in Jerusalem or minister to those who had not yet received the truth. Thus, when we see Paul having Timothy circumcised in Acts 16:3, we would not use that to prove God requires circumcision today. Or, when we see Paul enter the Temple after the ritual purification (even having an animal sacrifice offered for him), it does not mean that God requires animal sacrifices for us today. When we see Peter refusing to eat with Gentiles at various times, we would not say this is a requirement for today. And if we still see them water baptizing (required for entering the Temple and for any Gentile conversion), this does not prove that God requires this washing for us today, because we now have the New Covenant washing—the spiritual washing that the Lord Jesus provides.

God was leading these believers to understand that they were now in the promised New Covenant, showing that natural events under the law were pointing to spiritual truth in the Messiah's time. Therefore, the natural Passover lamb pointed forward, and now in the Book of Acts, the natural Feast of Pentecost gave way to the spiritual experience of Pentecost. And another part of this transition was moving from the natural baptism/washing in water to the promised spiritual washing that Jesus brought in—the Holy Spirit washing.

> ^{NIV} 1 Corinthians 15:46 The spiritual did not come first, but the natural, and after that the spiritual.

With all of these points in mind, it is at least possible that some of the baptism events listed in the Book of Acts may have been referring to the Spirit baptism/washing. Therefore, some points will be mentioned in certain events that show that **water** baptism may not have been the focus. Although all of these events in Acts could have indeed been water baptisms, yet when the baptism is not specified as water, it may have referred to the promised Holy Spirit washing that Jesus brought in. Either way, there was a gradual change-over into the New Covenant, and moving beyond the various water baptisms was a part of this transition:

> ^{NIV} Hebrews 9:10 They are only a matter of food and drink and various ceremonial washings—external regulations applying until the time of the new order.

9.6 ACTS 2: THE PROMISE OF THE FATHER

(See reasons 1–6, 11, and 12.)

The events in Acts 2 occurred at the second annual Feast of the Jews called Pentecost, where approximately 120 disciples were filled with the Holy Spirit of God (Acts 2:1–4). We spiritually fulfill the first feast—the Passover—when we receive the Messiah's baptism; this is the washing that comes from believing in the Messiah's shed blood and resurrection for forgiveness and salvation. Then we are ready to spiritually fulfill the second Feast—Pentecost—by being filled with God's Spirit.

> ^{NAS} Acts 2:4 And they were all **filled with the Holy Spirit** and began to speak with other tongues, as the Spirit was giving them utterance.

Peter says that this amazing event fulfilled what was prophesied by the prophet Joel—that a time was coming when God would pour out His spirit on all flesh (Acts 2:16-18). This was the promise of the Father. Prior to this event, God's Holy Spirit was given at rare times to high-ranking men like kings and prophets (see Exodus 31:2-3; Micah 3:5-8; Luke 1:67), but now it was available to any Israelite (both men and women) and even to Gentiles, as would happen later in Acts 10.

Yet, this event in Acts 2 is a totally different situation than what occurred with the baptism in Acts 10, which specifically mentioned a **water** baptism for those new Gentile believers. Here in Acts 2, no water is mentioned, possibly because Peter is now speaking to law-observant Jews who would have already been ritually clean to gather and appear at the Temple, as was required for this Feast day. Being ritually clean, they would have already had the necessary immersion/baptism in water that was required for gathering together at the Temple for Pentecost. Tradition has handed down to us that Acts 2:38 was another water baptism, but that does not necessarily make that belief correct.

Notice below that Peter says they need to be baptized in the name of Jesus "for the forgiveness of your sins." And **water** baptism is not what forgives sins. Believing in Jesus and the atonement that his shed blood provides (i.e., the Messiah's Spirit baptism) does that—not when we are ritually dipped in water. It is very possible that Peter, under God's anointing, was referring to the Messiah's washing/baptism here:

> NAS Acts 2:37-38 Now when they heard *this*, they were pierced to the heart, and said to Peter and the rest of the apostles, "Brethren, what shall we do?" And Peter *said* to them, "Repent, and **let each of you be baptized** in the name of Jesus Christ **for the forgiveness of your sins**; and you shall receive the gift of the Holy Spirit.

Peter had preached that Jesus was the promised son of David and what the religious leaders had done to him. These observant Jews were then pierced to the heart and wanted to know what to do. However, when Peter says to be washed/baptized in the name of Jesus for forgiveness, he may not be going backward to water baptism; it is at least possible that he is moving forward to the Spirit baptism the Messiah wanted. After all, Peter had just told them that Jesus received "from the Father the promise of the Holy Spirit" and that this, just poured forth on the disciples, is what they now see and hear:

> NAS Acts 2:33 "Therefore having been exalted to the right hand of God, and having received from the Father **the promise of the Holy Spirit,** He has **poured forth this** which **you both see and hear.**

This verse above shows that Peter understands that this is a spiritual "pouring forth," a spiritual baptism/washing and filling. So this may be speaking of believing in Jesus for cleansing and forgivingness and thus being spiritually baptized/washed. After believing in Jesus for salvation (the Spirit baptism), one is then prepared to receive the infilling of the Holy Spirit:

> NAS Acts 2:38 And Peter *said* to them, "Repent, and let each of you be baptized in the name of Jesus Christ for the forgiveness of your sins; **and you shall receive the gift of the Holy Spirit.**

If Peter means you have to repent and be **water** baptized for forgiveness (and to receive the Holy Spirit), then he would be wrong here, for God forgave and filled many with the Holy Spirit who were not water baptized (Acts 10:44–48). And God certainly does not fill unforgiven, unwashed, sin-burdened people with the Holy Spirit.

Peter says to repent and be baptized/washed in the name of Jesus and all that that name stood for (nothing says in water), and then you will receive the promised gift of the Holy Spirit. Thus, those who believed Peter's words concerning Jesus may have been spiritually washed (i.e., without water):

> NAS Acts 2:41 So then, **those who had received his word** were **baptized**; and there were added that day about three thousand souls.

As we saw earlier in chapter 3, baptizing in the name of Jesus does not refer to a ritualistic mode of how to water baptize someone (i.e., "I now baptize you in the name of Jesus") any more than "teaching in the name of Jesus" refers to someone who must ritually state before each sermon, "I now teach you in the name of Jesus." That is not what Acts 2:38 or Acts 4:18 meant when they said "in the name of Jesus":

> ^{NAS} Acts 4:18 And when they had summoned them, they commanded them not to speak or teach at all **in the name of Jesus**.

Teaching in the name of Jesus, speaking in the name of Jesus, and baptizing/washing/immersing in the name of Jesus can all refer to a teaching, speaking, or a washing (baptism) that has Christ as the source and subject of what is happening or being brought forth.

It must be remembered (as this book has shown) that first-century Jews did not have a Roman-style baptism in mind when they used this word. Peter says nothing of **water** baptism here. There was no lake nearby, the Jordan River was over fifteen miles away, and nothing says that these 3,000 ritually clean new believers in Jesus all lined up at a nearby *mikveh*.

Additionally, no proof exists that Jesus told the disciples that they would be bringing a new **water** baptism. In fact, both he and John always contrasted the water baptism to the **Spirit** baptism that he would bring in (Matthew 3:11; Mark 1:8; Luke 3:16; John 1:33; Acts 1:5; 11:16). So if Peter is bringing in a water baptism here, then he is doing it of his own accord, not yet having the New Covenant revelation as Paul came into.

Although the disciples of course already believed before this day, they did not receive the Messiah's baptism until Pentecost. For various reasons, the Messiah's promised Spirit baptism did not begin immediately after the resurrection but at Pentecost, just as Jesus said several days earlier:

> ^{NAS} Acts 1:5 for John baptized with water, **but** you shall be **baptized with the Holy Spirit** not many days from now."

The Messiah does **not** say here, "Oh, and I almost forgot, be sure to bring the new water baptism, with the new formula in my name." And as we have seen, that is not what Matthew 28:19 meant.

Those 120 gathered for Pentecost, including the apostles, not only received the baptism in the Holy Spirit (the Messiah's baptism/washing) on this day, but they also received the infilling of the Spirit (Acts 2:4) at the same time, just like the Gentiles did later in Acts 10:44–46.

One reason that the Messiah's baptism did not begin immediately after the resurrection is that he still walked among them in the flesh for 40 days. The scripture says that the Messiah became a life-giving spirit and this spiritual washing began at Pentecost, when they were also filled.

> NAS 1 Corinthians 15:45 So also it is written, "The first man, Adam, became a living soul." The last Adam *became* a life-giving spirit.

9.7 ACTS 8:12–17: THOSE IN SAMARIA ARE WASHED/BAPTIZED BY BELIEVING

(See reasons 1–6 and 11.)

Acts 8:12–17 has been somewhat covered already in this book, but here are some additional points to consider. First, we see that they were "being washed" when they believed Philip:

> NAS Acts 8:12 But **when they believed** Philip preaching the good news about the kingdom of God and the name of Jesus Christ, they were **being baptized**, men and women alike.

Since this does not say they were baptized **in water**, we again would have to determine if these apostles were now understanding the Messiah's Spirit baptism and bringing that forth, or if this was with water.

Nothing in the text requires that this means someone was washing/baptizing these women and men in water right as they believed. Young's Literal Translation does a better job of showing that they were spiritually baptized/washed at the moment they believed. Good translators never want to change the meaning of scripture, but they often add words or punctuation to the Greek to give the accurate meaning in English. I have added the parentheses (to the words that were there) in the verse below to give the sense of what is possibly being meant here—that when they believed, they were washed/baptized:

> ʸᴸᵀ Acts 8:12 And **when they believed Philip**, (proclaiming good news, the things concerning the reign of God and the name of Jesus Christ), **they were baptized both men and women**;

Simon was another one of these Samaritans who believed; he believed and was thus spiritually washed with the Messiah's washing. Knowing how the early Jews used this word, if we translate this to "Simon believed and was washed," it would make more sense:

> ᴺᴵⱽ Acts 8:13 Simon himself **believed and was baptized**. And he followed Philip everywhere, astonished by the great signs and miracles he saw.

And when the apostles heard that those in Samaria believed—and were thus washed/baptized in the name of Jesus (i.e., by his Spirit baptism)—their concern was to get the Samaritan believers filled with the Holy Spirit:

> ᴺᴬˢ Acts 8:14–17 Now when the apostles in Jerusalem heard that Samaria **had received the word of God**, they sent them Peter and John, who came down and prayed for them, that they might receive the Holy Spirit. **For He had not yet fallen upon any of them**; they had simply been **baptized in the name** of the Lord Jesus. Then they *began* laying their hands on them, **and they were receiving the Holy Spirit**.

So they had been ritually washed (baptized with the Messiah's Holy Spirit baptism, as he wanted) by believing in the Lord Jesus, but they had not yet received the infilling of the Holy Spirit. If this were indeed a water baptism in verse 12, it is probably because these apostles had not yet come into the same New Covenant understanding as Paul had. One more option would be that this was the water baptism that was required by the religious authorities in their day for Gentiles to be accepted as proselytes (see 2.7).

9.8 ACTS 8:38: THE WATER BAPTISM OF THE EUNUCH

(See reasons 1–6, 11, and 12.)

> NAS Acts 8:36–40 ³⁶And as they went along the road they came to some water; and the eunuch said, "Look! Water! What prevents me from being baptized?" ³⁷***And Philip said, "If you believe with all your heart, you may." And he answered and said, "I believe that Jesus Christ is the Son of God."*** ³⁸And he ordered the chariot to stop; and they both went down into the water, Philip as well as the eunuch; and he baptized him. ³⁹And when they came up out of the water, the Spirit of the Lord snatched Philip away; and the eunuch saw him no more, but went on his way rejoicing. ⁴⁰ But Philip found himself at Azotus; and as he passed through he kept preaching the gospel to all the cities, until he came to Caesarea.

First of all, notice above the verse that is italicized (which I boldfaced, verse 37). This italicizing means that it was not part of the original Greek scripture. It thus appears that a scribe may have wanted this to look more like a Christian baptism, so he added those words and they were accepted, even though they are not in the majority of Greek manuscripts (Bruce Metzger in his textual commentary says it "is a Western addition" [54]). So someone in the west (Rome) most likely wanted a clear confession of a faith-type statement before this supposed "Christian baptism" could be administered to this Gentile eunuch.

---

54 Metzger, *A Textual Commentary on the Greek New Testament*, p. 359.

132 THE MESSIAH'S BAPTISM

Notice also that it was the eunuch who brings up baptism/washing (not Philip). It was also the eunuch who ordered his own driver to stop the chariot at the water, not Philip (i.e., when you remove the spurious verse). So this again is possibly the common water baptism that a Gentile proselyte needed to undergo to be considered a ritually clean member of Israel's commonwealth. Phillip saw nothing wrong with it and obliged his request.

Whatever this instance may have been, some apostles did continue water baptizing after the resurrection and into the New Testament. Even Paul did it for a short time until he came to understand that Christ did not send him to water baptize. Water baptism was an ingrained part of Jewish purification since it was required at the Temple and for a Gentile to be considered clean. Thus, it is perfectly normal to continue seeing some water baptisms until the new paradigm and understanding fully came in.

This is especially so when you consider how they continued to meet daily in the Temple and how this was a meeting place for some years (Acts 2:46; 5:12; 21:26; 24:17-18), which required water baptisms/immersions for ritual cleansing before entering (as seen in chapter 2).

As we saw in the earlier section above, the disciples of Jesus were water baptizing (John 3:22, 23), but Jesus was not joining in with them (John 4:1).

9.9 ACTS 9 AND 22: THE SUPPOSED WATER BAPTISM OF PAUL

(See reasons 1-6 and 10-12.)

Acts 9 gives us the account where Paul (Saul) is "breathing threats and murders against the disciples," and the Lord appears to him on the road to Damascus, saying "Saul, Saul, why are you persecuting Me?" Saul is then blinded by this bright light from heaven and is led into the city still blind. Then the Lord Jesus appears to a disciple named Ananias in a vision and tells him to go to Paul and pray that he might regain his sight and be **filled with the Holy Spirit**:

> NAS Acts 9:17 And Ananias departed and entered the house, and after laying his hands on him said, "Brother Saul, the Lord Jesus, who appeared to you on the road by which you were coming, has sent me so that you may regain your sight, **and be filled with the Holy Spirit.**"

This of course fits perfectly with the premise of this book—that the Messiah wanted the Spirit baptism and infilling for the New Covenant, not a water baptism. Notice Ananias does **not** say "Oh, Saul, I almost forgot, the Lord Jesus also wants me to perform **a water baptism rite** for you, using a certain formula, so that you can be saved." No, we do not see the Lord tell Ananias to water baptize Paul, but instead to pray that he might be filled with the Holy Spirit, since that was what the Messiah was concerned with.

Now, for water baptism enthusiasts, the following verse is their hope:

> NAS Acts 9:18 And immediately there fell from his eyes something like scales, and he regained his sight, and **he arose and was baptized**;

But in the first-century Jewish idiom and in the Greek that was used here, this could just as easily read, "he arose washed" or "having risen, he was washed," where it referred to the New Covenant spiritual washing that Paul had received.

In Acts 22, Paul recounts this event and gives us additional proof that this was a spiritual washing, because it shows that when he accepted the words from Ananias, he arose and was washed as he called on the name of the Lord for cleansing; it was probably not a water baptism here.

Paul recounts this event:

> NAS Acts 22:12-16 "And a certain Ananias, a man who was devout by the standard of the Law, *and* well spoken of by all the Jews who lived there, came to me, and standing near

said to me, 'Brother Saul, receive your sight!' And at that very time I looked up at him. "And he said, **'The God of our fathers has appointed you to know His will**, and to see the Righteous One, and to hear an utterance from His mouth. 'For you will be a witness for Him to all men of what you have seen and heard. 'And now why do you delay? Arise, **and be baptized, and wash away your sins, calling on His name.'**

Now the Greek here is interesting in that the word for baptized is in the middle voice, so Ananias is probably meaning "arise, baptize/wash **yourself**," as Young's Literal Translation points out. Here is verse 16 again in their translation:

> YLT Acts 22:16   and now, why tarriest thou? having risen, **baptize thyself**, and **wash away thy sins, calling upon the name** of the Lord.

If we assume water baptism is what is being spoken of here, the man of God (Ananias) does not give accurate instruction. In Roman/Christian water baptism, nobody water baptizes *themselves* calling on the name of the Lord. According to a Roman water baptism (and the slightly changed Protestant water baptism that followed), a minister baptizes you using a prescribed formula—you never baptize yourself.

Therefore, this baptism of Paul is probably not a washing/baptism in water. The middle voice usage of the Greek word for baptism here is similar to where the Pharisee was troubled that Jesus had not first "baptized himself" before eating bread (Luke 11:38 in Greek [55]). There, it concerned natural water baptism/washing of the hands, and Jesus did not oblige, but here with Paul it is probably the Messiah's spirit washing.

Paul is told to "wash thyself" by calling upon the name of the Lord for cleansing and forgiveness, not by doing a water baptism. Remember,

---

55   The Greek scholar Lenski says that, concerning the Greek word for baptize in Luke 11:38, it is used "in the sense of the middle" voice here, where Jesus did not "wash himself" before the meal.

this is the New Covenant here and the Messiah's Spirit baptism is now available. In the New Covenant, we do not wash away our sins by a ritual bath/baptism. Paul said those baptisms are no longer imposed, nor are they effectual. Instead, we are washed and cleansed when we call upon his name for cleansing.

We "baptize/wash ourselves" (as Paul did above) by asking the Lord for cleansing and forgiveness, and we then arise washed just as Paul also did. And if this scripture is really true, that "the God of our fathers" has appointed Paul "to know His will," then Paul saying Christ did not send him to baptize (in water) shows he indeed did "know His will."

9.10 ACTS 16:13-15: THE BAPTISM/WASHING OF LYDIA AND HER HOUSEHOLD

(See reasons 1–10 and 12.)

The following scriptures may appear as though Paul is administering water baptism. However, since Paul emphatically states that Christ did not send him to baptize, then why would he be here water baptizing? These scriptures state that this woman and her household **believed** and were washed/baptized. It does not say they were **water** baptized, so we would want to remember Paul's claim to have baptized only a few (1 Corinthians 1:14–17). This woman and her household were not mentioned in Paul's letter to the Corinthians as ones he had water baptized. Here is the baptism with Lydia:

> NAS Acts 16:13–15 And on the Sabbath day we went outside the gate to a riverside, where we were supposing that there would be a place of prayer; and we sat down and began speaking to the women who had assembled. And a certain woman named Lydia, from the city of Thyatira, a seller of purple fabrics, a worshiper of God, was listening; **and the Lord opened her heart to respond to the things spoken by Paul. And when she and her household had been baptized**, she urged us, saying, "If you have judged me to be faithful to the Lord, come into my house and stay." And she prevailed upon us.

Again, using the Greek word for baptized in the New Covenant Jewish sense, this verse could easily be saying that she and her household responded to Paul's words and were "washed" and forgiven by believing. After this woman (a Gentile proselyte) was washed/baptized by believing in the Messiah, then Paul and Silas entered her house. In section 9.12, I show that this event with Lydia and her household as well as the next listed event (the prison baptism) occurred *after* Paul's letter to the Corinthians. Yet, when Paul lists the water baptisms he has done (1 Corinthians 1:14-17), he does not mention these, adding additional proof that these may have referred to spiritual washings.

9.11 ACTS 16:30-33: THE PRISON BAPTISM/WASHING STUMPS THE COMMENTATORS

(See reasons 1-10 and 12.)

On the surface, this looks like Paul is again administering water baptism. However, since Paul emphatically states that Christ did not send him to baptize, then why would he be here water baptizing? This is another set of scriptures that, when examined more closely in Greek while considering the Jewish idioms on "washed" and "baptized," a different picture emerges.

In the verses leading up to this event, a big earthquake occurs and then Paul and others have their prison doors opened and their chains unfastened. The jailer, knowing that this is supernatural, is in shock and cries out to Paul as to how he can be saved. Paul does **not say** it's by water baptism using the correct formula:

> NAS Acts 16:30-33 and after he brought them out, he said, **"Sirs, what must I do to be saved?"** And they said, **"Believe in the Lord Jesus,** and **you shall be saved**, you and your household." And they spoke the word of the Lord to him together with all who were in his house. And he took them that *very* hour of the night and washed their wounds, **and immediately he was baptized, he and all his** *household.*

When the jailer asks Paul and Silas what he must do to be saved, they reply that it's by believing in the Lord Jesus, and immediately the jailer and his household are *washed* by believing. This fits perfectly with the New Covenant Jewish usage of the word "baptism"—that when one believes in the Messiah, they are washed (baptized), cleansed, and thus saved. Paul does NOT say, "Oh my, I almost forgot, you also need to be **water baptized** using the correct formula, because you can't be saved without that."

Commentators who strongly believe in water baptism also agree that there is a problem here with this being a normal water baptism. Since this took place in a prison (in the Gentile city of Philippi, part of the Roman colony), it just does not have the look of a standard water baptism. They say that with no water for an immersion/baptism, there must have been some other way to administer baptism, and that must be what happened with Paul here. They are correct, because this was the New Covenant spiritual washing/baptism that occurs when one believes, so no water is needed for this washing.

To delve into this further, we will examine what two of these commentators say about Acts 16:32–33. First, Adam Clarke brings out the sense of the Greek word translated as "immediately" (verse 33), and he does not see how this can fit for a water baptism for their whole household in this Gentile prison:

Acts 16:32

And, by the way, if *he and all his were baptized straightway,* παραχηρημα, **immediately, instantly, at that very time,** *dum ipsa res agitur,* **it is by no means likely that there was any *immersion* in the case**; indeed, all the circumstances of the case, the dead of the night, the general agitation, the necessity of despatch, and the words of the text, all disprove it. **The apostles, therefore, had another method of administering baptism besides *immersion*,** which, if practiced according to the Jewish formalities, must have required considerable time, and not a little publicity.

It is therefore pretty evident that we have in this chapter very presumptive proofs:

1. That **baptism was administered without *immersion*,** as in the case of the jailor and his family; and
2. That children were also received into the church [56]

Other commentators like Barnes (also big on water baptism) express the same doubts, saying that this does not look like **water** baptism here:

> *And was baptized.* This was done *straightway*; that is, **immediately**. As it is altogether improbable that either in his house or in the prison there would be water sufficient for *immersing* them, there is every reason to suppose that **this was performed in some other mode**. All the circumstances lead us to suppose that it was not by immersion. It was at the dead of night; in a prison; amidst much agitation; and was evidently performed in haste. [57]

The reason that this does not look like a regular water baptism is because it most likely wasn't. These commentators are correct, but they might be missing the real reason why. It was probably because this was another instance of the Messiah's New Covenant baptism/washing that came by believing in the Messiah and his baptism/washing. In verse 32, the jailer and everyone in the household all believed, and verse 33 shows that they were immediately "washed" by believing.

This is just what Paul and Silas told them was the way to cleansing and salvation—not through a water baptism. Paul would not return to the Old Covenant immersions in water here because he knew those were no longer imposed by God. When the jailer asks how to be saved, Paul does not respond by saying that it's by water immersion but instead he says that it is by believing in the Lord Jesus.

---

56 Clarke, *Clarke's Commentary*, vol. 3, p. 819.
57 Barnes, *Barnes' Notes on the New Testament*, p. 479.

9.12 ACTS 19:1-7: THE BAPTISM/WASHING IN EPHESUS

(See reasons 1–12.)

This portion of scripture has been covered already to some degree (in section 5.5), but here are a few additional points as to why this may be referring to the Spirit washing (the Messiah's baptism):

> ^{NAS} Acts 19:1-7 And it came about that while Apollos was at Corinth, Paul having passed through the upper country came to Ephesus, and found some disciples, ²and he said to them, **"Did you receive the Holy Spirit when you believed?"** And they *said* to him, "No, we have not even heard whether there is a Holy Spirit." ³And he said, "Into what then were you baptized?" And they said, "Into John's baptism." ⁴And Paul said, "John baptized with the baptism of repentance, telling the people to believe in Him who was coming after him, that is, in Jesus." ⁵**And when they heard this, they were baptized in the name of the Lord Jesus.** ⁶And when Paul had laid his hands upon them, the Holy Spirit came on them, and they *began* speaking with tongues and prophesying. ⁷And there were in all about twelve men.

The backdrop for this baptism event is that Paul had previously spent eighteen months teaching in Corinth (Acts 18:11), and, while growing that church, he baptized only a handful of believers, firmly stating that Christ did not send him to baptize (1 Corinthians 1:14–17). So would it really make sense that when Paul is outside of Corinth (i.e., these events in Acts), he all of a sudden changes focus and water baptizes everyone he meets?

As we saw in the previous few sections, Paul supposedly water baptizes Lydia and her household (Acts 16:13–15), then the jailer and his entire household (Acts 16:30–33), and now this group of around twelve (possibly twenty to thirty people total in these events). Yet, when Paul wrote to the Corinthians stating that he baptized only a few people (because Christ did not call him to baptize), he does not mention any of these baptisms in Acts. Not only that, but after he names those few he did water baptize (saying it was because Christ did not send him to baptize), he then declares, "beyond that, I do not know whether I baptized any other" (1 Corinthians 1:16).

Yet, many scholars point out that Paul wrote that first epistle to the Corinthians at the end of his stay in Ephesus before leaving for Greece.[58][59] Since this Acts 19 event takes place just as Paul arrives in Ephesus, it is **before** he writes that first letter to the Corinthians. Therefore, when Paul defends his reason for baptizing only a few of them, he could have also mentioned all of these supposed Acts water baptisms in his list of those he had baptized. Yet, he mentions none of them.

Thus, when Paul writes to the Corinthians that he baptized only a few believers and leaves all of these other events in Acts off that list, it adds more credibility to the position that says some of these baptism/washings in Acts were probably not in water. Considering all of these facts, these baptisms are more likely referring to the one baptism Paul wrote of (Ephesians 4:5). After all, when he writes to the Corinthians, he already understood there was only one baptism and that it was the Messiah's promised Spirit baptism (1 Corinthians 12:13).

Remember, Paul often used a natural word when referring to something spiritual. As was covered in the natural-to-spiritual section (chapter 4), we would not search for the lost altar of Paul based on the following verse, because Paul was speaking spiritually, referring to a *spiritual* altar:

> [NAS] Hebrews 13:10 **We have an altar**, from which those who serve the tabernacle have no right to eat.

Neither should we seek "pure water" to have our bodies washed with based on this verse, for this also is meant spiritually:

> [NAS] Hebrews 10:22 let us draw near with a sincere heart in full assurance of faith, having our hearts sprinkled *clean*

---

58 Clarke, *Clarke's Commentary*, vol. 3, section 2, p. 182.
59 Jamieson, Fausset, and Brown, *A Commentary*, vol. 3, p. vi.

from an evil conscience and **our bodies washed with pure water.**

In Rome, the focus turned to water baptism, and the Messiah's Spirit baptism was all but forgotten. But the same cannot be said for Paul; the scripture below shows that he fully understood that in the New Covenant, the one baptism was the Holy Spirit washing. Here again, he uses the word for baptism in its spiritual sense:

> NIV 1 Corinthians 12:13   For we were all **baptized by one Spirit** into one body—whether Jews or Greeks, slave or free—**and** we were all given the one Spirit to drink.

What we see Paul concerned about in Acts 19, when he first thinks that this group already believes in Jesus, is if they received the Holy Spirit when they believed (Acts 19:2). Yet, right after they believe in Jesus, instead of praying that they then receive the Holy Spirit, are we to assume that Paul immediately takes them somewhere suitable for a water baptism? Then, after that supposed water baptism takes place (while everyone was possibly still dripping wet), he then prays for them to receive the Holy Spirit (verse 6)?

It is possible that Paul sought out and found water to baptize these believers (we do not know if water was near or far away at that point). However, when seen through the Jewish idiom of the day, this verse could just as well be saying that they were "washed" (baptized) spiritually in the name of Jesus (and everything his name referred to) right when they believed:

> NAS Acts 19:5   And **when they heard** this, **they were baptized** in the name of the Lord Jesus.

The Greek literally says that they were baptized/washed "**into** the name of the Lord Jesus."

Would Paul defend himself for having baptized only a few people in Corinth, strongly affirming that Christ did not send him to baptize, only to turn around when outside Corinth and water baptize people left and right? Or would it make more sense that some of these baptisms were the promised Holy Spirit baptisms and that the recipients were spiritually washed when they believed?

In light of Paul's teachings, even if these were all baptisms in water (which is doubtful when considering all of the evidence), it was only because this was a time of transition as the Holy Spirit was leading them into New Covenant truth (as expressed in section 9.5).

9.13 ACTS 22:16

(See section 9.9 above: "Acts 9 and 22: The Supposed Water Baptism of Paul.")

9.14 1 CORINTHIANS 15:29: BAPTIZED FOR THE DEAD ONES

(See reasons 5–10 and 12.)

This verse has been difficult for commentators for many years, with Adam Clarke calling it the most difficult verse in the New Testament. One commentary said that up to 200 explanations have been given for this verse! So here I go with explanation 201.

First, remember that Paul thanks God that he baptized only a few people, because Christ did not send him to baptize. Paul is not teaching the essentials of water baptism here.

Some commentators, like Tertullian, actually believe these were water baptisms done for dead people (like the Mormons do), who had not had a chance to be water baptized while alive. But would Paul use some lame argument, referencing something about an offshoot sect, to somehow support his arguments on the resurrection (which is the context here)? Here is the verse in question (29), with two other verses added for context:

> [NAS] 1 Corinthians 15:12 Now if Christ is preached, that He has been raised from the dead, **how do some among you say that there is no resurrection of the dead?**

9. Some Additional Baptism Scriptures Explained 143

^{NAS} 1 Corinthians 15:29 Otherwise, what will **those do who are baptized for the dead? If the dead are not raised** at all, why then are they baptized for them?

^{NAS} 1 Corinthians 15:32 If from human motives I fought with wild beasts at Ephesus, what does it profit me? **If the dead are not raised,** let us eat and drink, for tomorrow we die.

In verse 29, the two Greek words translated as "dead" are both plural. Paul asks what will "those" do, not "we," because he is not among "those" who still believe in water baptizing.

Many people from diverse backgrounds were coming to know the Lord, and they would bring their beliefs with them. As we know, people are often very reluctant to give up on the traditions of man, which is why Jesus warned against them (Mark 7:7–8). The Sadducees did not believe in the resurrection (Acts 23:8), and a great many of the priests (Sadducees, from Zadok) had come to know the Messiah (Acts 6:7). Some disciples of John were apparently continuing with his water baptism, such as those Paul came across (Acts 19:1–6). With no Internet, television, and other modern media, truth often traveled slowly. Different disciples had different understandings, depending on their backgrounds and what teaching they had received.

In 1 Corinthians 15:29, Paul could be pointing out that the same disciples who argue that there is no resurrection are also those who still continue various water baptisms (those into John and those into Jesus). And, speaking from the Jewish understanding of ritual purification, Paul says that if the dead ones (plural, i.e., Jesus and John) are not resurrected into heaven, then why are they being baptized/washed into them? In other words, you are not washed or ritually cleansed by those who are still dead, because in the Jewish idiom, dead people made one unclean, not ritually clean.

9.15 ROMANS 6:3-5, GALATIANS 3:27, AND COLOSSIANS 2:12: BAPTIZED INTO THE MESSIAH'S DEATH

(See reasons 1 through 12.)

The following scriptures will all be covered together because they are all on the similar subject of being baptized/washed into Christ's death and being raised with him through his resurrection to walk in the newness of life:

> ^{NAS} Romans 6:3 Or do you not know that all of us who have been **baptized into Christ** Jesus **have been baptized into His death?**

> ^{NAS} Romans 6:4 Therefore **we have been buried with Him through baptism into death**, in order that as Christ was raised from the dead through the glory of the Father, so **we too might walk in newness of life.**

> ^{NAS} Romans 6:5 For if we have become united with *Him* in the likeness of His death, certainly we shall be also *in the likeness* of His resurrection,

> ^{NAS} Galatians 3:27 For all of you who were baptized into Christ have clothed yourselves with Christ.

> ^{NIV} Colossians 2:11–13 ¹¹ In him you were also circumcised, in the putting off of the sinful nature, not with a circumcision done by the hands of men but with the circumcision done by Christ, ¹² having been buried with him in baptism and raised with him through your faith in the power of God, who raised him from the dead. ¹³ When you were dead in your sins and in the uncircumcision of your sinful nature, God made you alive with Christ. He forgave us all our sins,

The Galatians 3:27 verse listed above is the easy one, so let's consider it first. Paul here is speaking about the one baptism, the Spirit baptism; we are clothed with Christ when we receive the Holy Spirit baptism Jesus provides:

> ^{NAS} 1 Corinthians 12:13 For **by one Spirit we were all baptized** into one body, whether Jews or Greeks, whether slaves or free, and we were all made to drink of one Spirit.

Paul, who thanked God that he no longer baptized because Christ did not send him to baptize (1 Corinthians 1:14–17) and wrote that it was no longer imposed by God (Hebrews 9:10, where the word translated as "washings" by most translations is "baptisms" in Greek), is not all of a sudden overturning all that teaching to now speak in these scriptures on the merits of **water** baptism.

If we have water-baptism glasses on, we may see these scriptures with a view to a human tradition that has been handed down for centuries and extols **water** baptism. However, these scriptures connect baptism to Christ's death and burial, and Jewish burials never took place in water.

Obviously, these verses are not speaking about being buried in a water baptism. Our old self does not die, nor is it buried at a water baptism. Rather, it is when we accept Christ for our salvation (i.e., the Messiah's baptism/washing), and that is the context of these verses:

> ^{NAS} Romans 6:6–7 knowing this, that **our old self** was crucified with *Him*, that our body of sin might be done away with, that we should no longer be slaves to sin; for he who has died is freed from sin.

When we believe and accept salvation through Christ's atoning work, it is then that we walk in "newness of life" through his resurrection. That is when our "old self" is considered to be dead and buried—not at some later date, such as after a water baptism. Our old self (or "old man" in some translations) is to be considered as dead when we believe and become a new creation in him:

> ᴺᴬˢ Romans 6:11 Even so **consider yourselves to be dead to sin**, but alive to God **in** Christ Jesus.

It is not an immersion in water that causes us to be "clothed with Christ" (Galatians 3:27); rather, it is the Messiah's Spirit baptism (the only baptism still in effect, Hebrews 9:10) that comes when we accept his shed blood for our salvation. And the "In him you were also circumcised, in the putting off of the sinful nature" (Colossians 2:11 above) also happens when we are washed/baptized by believing in his forgiveness; this is the Messiah's Spirit baptism, and this is what was promised.

Since we know that Paul said there was only one baptism—the Spirit baptism (Ephesians 4:5; 1 Corinthians 12:13)—it would make far more sense that Paul is again speaking about the Messiah's baptism here.

Paul is not teaching the Romans that dipping in a water baptism is like dying and being buried in the earth. As was mentioned, first-century Jews did not bury their dead in water, so that's not what Paul means here. Instead, this illustrates that when we are washed/baptized from our sin *by believing* and are given a new cleansed spirit by God, with Christ dwelling within, our old sinful man is to be considered as dead and buried (Romans 6:11 above). And we are to be considered as raised through faith into a new creation. Remember that God filled the uncircumcised Gentiles with the Holy Spirit right after they believed (Acts 10:44-46), and no water baptism rite had been performed yet. God does not fill those who are still dead in sin with His Holy Spirit, so therefore the Gentiles' cleansing came only when they believed.

Jesus said that if he does not go away, the Holy Spirit (and thus his baptism) would not come (John 16:7 and John 7:37-39). This, of course, fits the type also, for if the Passover does not occur (with Christ paying the price), there would be no Pentecost to follow. Or, speaking spiritually, if there were no Passover Lamb of God and no first fruits offering (the Resurrection), then Pentecost could not spiritually come. Even speaking in the natural idiom without Passover and the first fruits offering, there would be nothing to count from for the 50-day count to Pentecost.

The whole purpose of the Messiah's death was that we might receive his baptism/washing and to be fully cleansed and receive the spiritual life from above:

> ^{NAS} 1 Peter 3:18 For **Christ also died for sins once for all**, *the* just for *the* unjust, in order that He might bring us to God, having been **put to death in the flesh**, but **made alive in the spirit**;

> ^{KJV} 2 Corinthians 5:17 Therefore if any man *be* in Christ, *he is* a new creature: **old things are passed away**; behold, all things are become new.

> ^{NAS} Romans 10:9 that if you confess with your mouth Jesus *as* Lord, and believe in your heart that God raised Him from the dead, you shall be saved;

9.16 HEBREWS 6:1-2: MOVING BEYOND THE TEACHING ON BAPTISMS/WASHINGS

(See reasons 1 through 12, because Paul's instruction on baptism concerned all of them.)

> ^{NAS} Hebrews 6:1-2 Therefore leaving the elementary teaching about the Christ, let us press on to maturity, not laying again a foundation of repentance from dead works and of faith toward God, **of instruction about washings**, and laying on of hands, and the resurrection of the dead, and eternal judgment.

The King James Translation translates verse 2 this way:

> ^{KJV} Hebrews 6:2 Of the **doctrine of baptisms**, and of laying on of hands, and of resurrection of the dead, and of eternal judgment.

In Hebrews 5, Paul had been speaking about the strong meat of God's word (such as the things about Melchizedek), but then Paul says they are not ready for such teachings and are more like babes needing milk. This theme continues here in chapter 6. When Paul mentions the basic doctrine of washings/baptisms, he is not saying that the two baptisms—water baptism and Spirit baptism teachings—were both to continue. He already made it very clear that there was just one baptism to be continued, and that was the Spirit baptism (Ephesians 4:5; 1 Corinthians 12:13; Hebrews 9:10).

It is the teaching on the natural baptisms (plural) in water that we are to move beyond. And this would begin with John's baptism, explaining that it was a baptism of repentance, and that John pointed ahead to Jesus (as Paul taught, Acts 19:1–6). From there it would follow that other various water baptisms would no longer be imposed in the New Covenant (as Paul came to understand and teach, Hebrews 9:10). When Paul understood the revelation that Christ did not send him to baptize, he moved beyond natural water baptisms.

Many don't like the idea of Paul saying that we are to leave behind the doctrine of baptisms, for they believe that we are never to go beyond this water baptism rite and are certain that it is a major command of God. They believe that only the Jewish instructions on "washings" are what we are to go beyond, but certainly not the sacrament of water baptism as a whole.

Young's Literal Translation is another translation that contains the word "baptisms" here, as an elementary teaching we are to move beyond:

> YLT Hebrews 6:2 of the teaching of **baptisms**, of laying on also of hands, of rising again also of the dead, and of judgment age-during,

It is the teachings on the natural washings in water that we move beyond in the New Covenant, and that is what Paul understood. The "teaching of baptisms" refers to the fact that the Messiah's Spirit baptism fulfilled the various water baptisms that are no longer required in the New Covenant (Hebrews 9:10).

9.17 CONCLUSION OF THE MATTER

In the introduction, we read the history of how Rome had seven sacraments and that when the Protestants departed Catholicism, they dropped five of these sacraments but accidentally took along the remaining two—the Blessed Eucharist (also called "Holy Communion") and water baptism. My first book, *The Messianic Feast: Moving Beyond the Ritual*, gave proof that the sacrament of the Blessed Eucharist was not something the Messiah wanted or taught. Instead, Jesus was speaking in parables at his last meal, which he intended for us to understand. And I believe this book has shown that the final sacrament, water baptism, was not the baptism/washing the Messiah wanted, nor was a water baptism ever imposed by God for believers in the New Covenant.

Here is a good question for us to consider: Will we test these last two sacraments, to be like the noble believers in Berea, who searched the scriptures to test and prove the various doctrines (Acts 17:10-11), or will the traditions of man that Jesus warned against win out?

> NAS Mark 7:7-8 'But in vain do they worship Me, Teaching as doctrines the precepts of men.' "Neglecting the commandment of God, you hold to the tradition of men."

Perhaps we should choose to join with Paul and admit that Christ did not send us to baptize in water? Either way, our main focus should be on the Messiah's baptism and the Holy Spirit infilling.

The Lord Jesus received the promise of the Father and he wants us to receive this free gift. His focus was always on the Spirit baptism that he would provide and the infilling of God's Spirit that would follow. In the New Covenant, this is what he pours forth:

> NAS Acts 2:33 "Therefore having been exalted to the right hand of God, and having received from the Father the promise of the Holy Spirit, He has poured forth this which you both see and hear.

10

Questions and Answers

Question: When I was water baptized, I had a powerful experience with God; how can you possibly believe that water baptism is not from Him?

Answer: It is not the purpose of this book to question your experience with God, and it is understood that others have had similar experiences during water baptism. When someone feels that God requires them to do something and then they do it, the expectation of being blessed by Him can be the very impetus that brings about such an experience. For example, some Catholics have testified to feeling God's presence mightily while using rosary beads, but this would not make the rosary a command from God. Almost any time a believer opens up to God, He is there to anoint and bless, even if our doctrine is not correct.

Question: Our church holds monthly baptism services where new believers publicly declare their faith before God and man. It is a very special time. Are you trying to end our special time at the baptism services?

Answer: Water baptism is a special service in many churches, and it is not the goal of this book to deny these times of fellowship to believers. However, according to the Lord Jesus, the apostles, and various scriptures, the truth is very important (John 16:13; Proverbs 23:23; 1 Timothy 4:16). If water baptism is a commandment from God for believers today, then we should practice it. Yet, if it is not, then believers have a right to know where God's heart lies on the matter.

Question: I was always taught that water baptism was the answer to having a good conscience before God, as the following verse relates:

> ^{NAS} 1 Peter 3:21   And corresponding to that, **baptism now saves you**—not the removal of dirt from the flesh, **but an appeal to God for a good conscience**—through the resurrection of Jesus Christ,

Answer: This would be true only if God required water baptism for us today. And the "baptism" in the verse above cannot be referring to *water* because this same verse says baptism **now saves you**. Since the scriptures say that water baptism is not what saves us (see sections 7.1, 7.2, 9.3, and 9.16 in this book), we therefore know that Peter was speaking about the Holy Spirit baptism the Messiah brought in. It is the Spirit baptism that now saves us and is the answer to a good conscience to God through the resurrection of Jesus.

Question: In our church, water baptism is a public confession of faith, as the Lord wanted. Isn't that what this verse says?

> ^{NAS} Matthew 10:32   "Everyone therefore who shall confess Me before men, I will also confess him before My Father who is in heaven.

Answer: If water baptism were the public confession that the Lord Jesus desired, then shouldn't he have told us that at least once in the scriptures? If the Lord intended for water baptism to fulfill this verse, then why not conduct water baptism services once a week, where **every** believer confesses his faith during it? If people tell you that they were water baptized in 1980 but have not said another word for the Lord since then, have they really fulfilled what Jesus meant about confessing him to men? Is it not better fulfilled by walking with the Lord day by day and not hiding our light before men? Is water baptism really a public confession when the service is sheltered away in church, where the public won't see it? Does that one dip in water in 1980 really fulfill what the Lord wanted when he said to confess him before men?

Question: I do believe that water baptism is not what saves us, and that salvation comes by believing in Jesus and appropriating his shed blood for forgiveness. However, I think water baptism is an important tradition and a big part of our religious heritage.

Answer: It is important to remember that Jesus warned about traditions of man that make the word of God of no effect (Matthew 15:3, 6; Mark 7:8-9). If water baptism is not a commandment from God, but we imply that it is, then having all new converts baptized in water changes the picture of what God's will is. It makes His word void by shifting the focus of what God and the Messiah wanted (the Holy Spirit baptism) and turns it back into a religious rite that is a tradition of man. Hence, water baptism portrays that God still wants us to do various deeds to have a good conscience instead of accepting and appropriating the Messiah's true washing. In effect, by holding to this tradition of man, we show to the world that God wants rituals instead of spirit and truth.

Question: I know your type! You need to get back to the Christian faith that has been handed down from the time of the Church Fathers. My Bible says that in the last days, some will depart from the faith and be deceived by doctrines of demons (1 Timothy 4:1). That scripture was written for people like you who do not follow the church doctrines that have been handed down for centuries!

Answer: That verse in Timothy concerning false doctrines in the last days is a very important scripture to remember any time we consider a Bible truth. We should make sure that every truth truly aligns with the scriptures and with what Jesus and the apostles taught. The scriptures clearly state that we are built upon the foundation of the apostles and prophets with Christ Jesus as the chief cornerstone (Ephesians 2:20). Nowhere in the Bible does it say that we are to be built upon those who men call "Church Fathers." Thus, the words of Paul on water baptism are infinitely more important than the words of Tertullian.

Also, concerning the deception in the last days of which Timothy speaks, the scriptures also show that God will pour out His Spirit during that same period:

> ^{NAS} Acts 2:17 'And it shall be **in the last days**,' God says, 'That I will pour forth of My Spirit upon all mankind; And your sons and your daughters shall prophesy, And your young men shall see visions, And your old men shall dream dreams;

The Bible also expresses that there will be a latter rain where God pours out His Spirit like rain, bringing His teaching. The believers would not need a teaching rain in the last days if they already had the full truth all along, since Roman times:

> ^{NAS} James 5:7 Be patient, therefore, brethren, until the coming of the Lord. Behold, the farmer waits for the precious produce of the soil, being patient about it, **until it gets the early and late rains.**

> ^{NAB} Joel 2:23 And do you, O children of Zion, exult and rejoice in the LORD, your God! He has given you **the teacher of justice**: he has made the rain come down for you, **the early and the late rain as before.**

> ^{NIV} Deuteronomy 32:2 **Let my teaching fall like rain** and my words descend like dew, like showers on new grass, like abundant rain on tender plants.

> ^{NAS} Isaiah 2:2-3 Now it will come about that **In the last days,** The mountain of the house of the LORD Will be established as the chief of the mountains, And will be raised above the hills; And all the nations will stream to it. And many peoples will come and say, "Come, let us go up to the mountain of the LORD, To the house of the God of Jacob;

> **That He may teach us** concerning His ways, And that we may walk in His paths."

Although this following verse addresses Daniel, it also shows that some Bible truths will be revealed in the last days:

> ᴺᴬˢ Daniel 12:4 "But as for you, Daniel, conceal these words and seal up the book until the end of time; many will go back and forth, and knowledge will increase."

> ᴺᴬˢ Daniel 12:9 And he said, "Go *your way*, Daniel, for *these* words **are concealed and sealed up until the end time.**

Believers have been slowly moving away from certain nonbiblical Roman teachings for the last few hundred years. During that period, Protestants dropped several Catholic doctrines that the mainstream Church believed for centuries (like transubstantiation, indulgences, salvation by works, penance, water baptism by sprinkling, etc.). So, Christians should not be surprised if we believers are still not perfectly founded on the pure doctrines of Jesus and the apostles. Indeed, the latter rain of God's Spirit and teaching will bring many scripture truths to light.

Question: I have committed some bad sins, and although I have accepted the Lord, I don't feel washed or cleansed.

Answer: God said that He would cast our sin away as far as the east is from the west, never to remember them against us (Psalm 103:12; Jeremiah 31:34). We might remember our sin, but we are legally cleansed and washed in God's sight. So we want to do our best to believe His word and in His promises of forgiveness and cleansing. So it essentially becomes "God said it, I believe it, and that settles it."

> ᴷᴶⱽ 1 John 1:9 If we confess our sins, he is faithful and just to forgive us *our* sins, and to cleanse us from all unrighteousness.

Index of Baptism Scriptures

This index lists the more important baptism-related scriptures, including the chapter and subheading (numbers) where that particular scripture is covered in this book.

Several scriptures are listed in which the English word for baptize (or baptism) does **not** appear in most translations, even though it is in the original Greek text. In these cases, most translations translate the Greek word for baptize into English as "wash" or "washing," possibly because to them it looks like a "Jewish ceremonial washing" (Luke 11:38; Mark 7:4), and they don't believe Jewish ceremonial washing should be connected to the Christian baptism.

Or, as in the case of Hebrews 9:10, most translators did not intend their translations to state that the various baptisms are "regulations for the body that are no longer imposed," as Paul said (in Greek). Most translators were fine with writing that the various "washings" were no longer imposed, but they didn't want to say that the various "baptisms" were not imposed. I am not at all trying to imply that the translators were dishonest, because there is certainly nothing wrong with translating the Greek word for baptism as "washing."

What I am saying is that the translators believed that water baptism was a rite commended by the Lord, and they therefore try to portray some baptisms as Jewish washings and others as the Christian rite of baptism. However, in the idiom of first-century Jews, there was no such difference in how the actual word was used. To them, the word primarily meant "wash," "washed," or "washing," and in the New Covenant, they often used it for the *spiritual* washing—the Messiah's Holy Spirit baptism/washing.

This index lists the chapter and subheading where baptism-related scriptures are covered in this book, listed here in order of occurrence in the Bible.

OLD TESTAMENT SCRIPTURES

Exodus 30:20	See 2.5; 3.3; 4.3.
Leviticus 14:8	See 2.5.
Leviticus 15:13	See 3.2.
Numbers 19:19	See 2.5.
2 Kings 5:14	See 2.1.
Isaiah 28:11–12	See 8.1; 8.3; 8.6.
Ezekiel 36:26–27	See 8.1.
Joel 2:28	See 3.2; 8.1.
Zechariah 13:1	See 3.2.
Malachi 3:1–5	See 2.2.

NEW TESTAMENT SCRIPTURES ON BAPTISM

Matthew 3:6	See 2.3.
Matthew 3:7	See 2.3.
Matthew 3:11	See 3.1.
Matthew 3:13	See 9.2.
Matthew 3:14	See 9.2.
Matthew 3:16	See 9.2.
Matthew 20:22	See the note below.
Matthew 20:23	See the note below.

With the two scriptures above, the Greek phrase that includes the baptism words is not in the better Greek manuscripts; it was likely copied over from Mark 10:38 by a copyist, where this phrase is original.

Matthew 28:19	See 3.5–7; 5.3.
Mark 1:8	See 3.1; 8.1; 9.1, Reason 2.
Mark 1:9	See 9.2.
Mark 7:2–4	See 2.1; 5.2.

Most translations say "washing" (of cups, etc.) in verse 4; the Greek word is "baptisms."

> YLT Mark 7.4 and, *coming* from the market-place, if they do not baptize themselves, they do not eat; and many other things there are that they received to hold, **baptisms** of cups, and pots, and brazen vessels, and couches.

Mark 7:7–8 See 8.8; 9.14; 9.17.

The word for baptism is probably not in the actual Greek of Mark 7:8. Although Young's Literal Translation includes the word "baptism" here, the best manuscripts do not have the Greek word for baptism in verse 8, and Metzger[60] believes it was a scribal addition from verse 4.

> YLT Mark 7:8 for, having put away the command of God, ye hold the tradition of men, **baptisms** of pots and cups; and many other such like things ye do.'

Mark 10:38 See 5.2; 7.4.
Mark 10:39 See 7.4.
Mark 16:9–20 See 3.6. (Concerning the long ending for Mark)
Mark 16:16 See 5.5.

---

60 Metzger, *A Textual Commentary on the Greek New Testament*, p. 94.

Luke 1:17, 23	See 2.2.
Luke 3:16	See 2.2; 3.1.
Luke 11:38	See 5.2; 5.5; 9.9.

This verse is another one of those that most translations have as "wash" (although the Greek word is "baptize"). Young's Literal Translation is the only one I saw that has "baptize":

> YLT Luke 11:38 and the Pharisee having seen, did wonder that he did not first **baptize himself** before the dinner.

Luke 11:39	See 5.5.
Luke 12:50	See 4.3; 7.4.
Luke 24:47	See 3.6
Luke 24:49	See 5.1; 8.1.
John 1:25	See 2.2.
John 1:31	See 2.2.
John 1:33	See 3.1; 8.1.
John 2:6	See 3.3; 5.5.
John 3:1–8	See 6.5; 8.1; 9.3.

Although the word for baptism is not in John 3:3–8, some argue that these verses teach "baptismal regeneration," so I cover them in 9.3.

John 3:22	See 3.1; 9.4.
John 3:23	See 3.1; 9.4.
John 3:26	See 3.1; 9.4.
John 4:1	See 3.1; 9.4.

John 4:2	See 3.1; 9.4.
John 4:7–14	See 8.2.
John 7:37–40	See 8.2.
John 11:55	See 2.3; 5.5.
John 13:10	See 3.3.
John 15:3	See 3.3.
Acts 1:5	See 3.1; 8.1; 9.6.
Acts 2:4	See 5.1; 8.1; 8.4; 9.6.
Acts 2:5–10	See 2.7.
Acts 2:33	See 5.1; 8.1; 8.4; 9.6.
Acts 2:38	See 8.1; 9.6.
Acts 2:41	See 9.6.
Acts 8:12	See 8.1; 8.5; 9.7.
Acts 8:13	See 9.7.
Acts 8:14–17	See 3.7; 8.1; 8.5; 9.7.
Acts 8:18–20	See 8.5.
Acts 8:36	See 9.8.
Acts 8:38	See 9.8.
Acts 9:17	See 6.3; 8.1.
Acts 9:18	See 9.9.
Acts 10:44–47	See 2.7; 6.4; 8.1.
Acts 10:48	See 2.7.
Acts 11:15–16	See 3.1; 3.5; 5.2.
Acts 16:15	See 9.10.
Acts 16:33	See 9.11.
Acts 18:8	See 6.1; 8.5.
Acts 19:1–7	See 3.7; 5.3; 5.5; 6.1; 8.1; 8.5; 9.12.
Acts 21:24–26	See 2.6.
Acts 22:16	See 9.9.
Romans 6:3	See 9.15.
Romans 6:4	See 9.15.
1 Corinthians 1:11	See 6.2.

1 Corinthians 1:13	See 6.2.
1 Corinthians 1:14	See 3.1; 6.1–3; 6.5.
1 Corinthians 1:15	See 6.1–3; 6.5.
1 Corinthians 1:16	See 6.3; 6.5.
1 Corinthians 1:17	See 3.1; 5.6; 6.3; 6.5.
1 Corinthians 6:11	See 3.7; 4.3; 5.1.
1 Corinthians 10:2	See 2.7; 6.1; 7.4.
1 Corinthians 12:13	See 3.5; 4.3; 5.1; 6.4.
1 Corinthians 15:29	See 9.14.
Galatians 3:27	See 9.15.
Ephesians 4:5	See 5.4; 9.1, Reason 10.
Ephesians 5:25–26	See 3.3; 4.3.
Colossians 2:12	See 9.15.
Titus 3:5	See 3.4; 4.3.
Hebrews 6:2	See 9.16.
Hebrews 9:9–10	See 2.7; 3.3; 5.1; 6.4; 7.3.

Hebrews 9:10 is another verse (like Mark 7:4 and Luke 11:38) where the Greek word for baptize/baptism/baptisms is usually translated into English as "washings" (or "wash," etc.). Young's Literal Translation is a rare translation that translates the Greek word for baptisms into English as "baptisms" here. Many translations want to use the word for washings here, probably to portray that it was only the Jewish ritual washings were no longer imposed, not the Christian baptism:

^{YLT} Hebrews 9:10 only in victuals, and drinks, and different **baptisms, and fleshly ordinances—till the time of reformation imposed upon *them*.**

This book has shown that there is, of course, nothing wrong with translating the Greek words for baptize and baptism as "wash" or "washing," but one has to be careful to not make a distinction between the first-century Jewish baptisms/washings and the supposed Christian baptism/washings (in water) where there may not have been one.

Hebrews 10:22	See 4.3; 5.1.
1 Peter 3:21	See 7.1–4.
1 John 1:7	See 3.4; 5.1.
1 John 1:9	See 3.4.

Bibliography

American-Israeli Cooperative Enterprise, Jewishvirtuallibrary.org, "Jewish Practices & Rituals: Mikveh," accessed November 29, 2016, https://www.jewishvirtuallibrary.org/jsource/Judaism/mikveh.html.

Barnes, Albert. *Barnes' Notes on the New Testament*. Edited by Ingram Cobbin. Grand Rapids, MI: Kregel Publications, 1962.

Clarke, Adam. *Clarke's Commentary*. Vol. 3, *Matthew–Revelation*. Nashville, TN: Abingdon Press, 1977.

Encyclopedia Judaica Research Foundation. *Encyclopedia Judaica*. Jerusalem: Keter Publishing House, 1972.

Herbermann, Charles G., Edward A. Pace, Condé B. Pallen, Thomas J. Shahan, and John J. Wynne. *The Catholic Encyclopedia*. New York: Robert Appleton Company, 1907–1912.

Jamieson, Robert, A. R. Fausset, and David Brown. *A Commentary, Critical, Experimental, and Practical, on the Old and New Testaments*. Grand Rapids, MI: Wm. B. Eerdmans Publishing, 1978.

The Jewish Encyclopedia. 12 vols. New York: Funk & Wagnalls Company, 1901.

Lenski, R. C. H. *Commentary on the New Testament: The Interpretation of St. Matthew's Gospel 15–28*. Minneapolis, MN: Augsburg Publishing House, 1964.

Maimonides, Moses. *The Guide for the Perplexed*. Translated by M. Friedländer. 2nd ed. London: Routledge & Kegan Paul, 1904. http://sacred-texts.com/jud/gfp/index.htm.

Metzger, Bruce M. *A Textual Commentary on the Greek New Testament: A Companion Volume to the United Bible Societies' Greek New Testament*. 3rd ed. London: United Bible Societies, 1975.

Roberts, Alexander, and James Donaldson, eds. *Ante-Nicene Fathers*. Vol. 3, *Latin Christianity: Its Founder: Tertullian; The Writings of the Fathers down to A.D. 325*. With revisions by A. Cleveland Coxe. Grand Rapids, MI: Wm. B. Eerdmans Publishing, 1993.

Schaff, Philip, and Henry Wace, eds. *Nicene and Post-Nicene Fathers*. Second Series, Vol. 3, *Theodoret, Jerome, Gennadius, Rufinus: Historical Writings, Etc*. Peabody, MA: Hendrickson Publishers, 1995.

Tennent, T. Alex, *The Messianic Feast: Moving Beyond the Ritual*. Seattle: Messianic Publishing, 2014.

Thayer, Joseph, *The New Thayer's Greek-English Lexicon of the New Testament*. Christian Copyrights, Inc., 1979.

Theopedia.com, s.v. "Biblical typology," accessed August 11, 2017, http://www.theopedia.com/Biblical_typology.

United Bible Societies. *A Concise Greek-English Dictionary of the New Testament* (known widely as *UBS Greek-English Dictionary*), incorporated inside *The Greek New Testament*, 3rd corrected ed. United Bible Societies: Stuttgart, 1983.

Wallace, Daniel B. *Greek Grammar Beyond the Basics: An Exegetical Syntax of the New Testament*. Grand Rapids, MI: Zondervan, 1996.

Yonge, Charles Duke. *The Works of Philo Judaeus*. Vol. 1. (London: H. G. Bohn, 1854–1890.) http://www.earlyjewishwritings.com/text/philo/book27.html.

Permissions

BWHEBB, BWHEBL, BWTRANSH [Hebrew]; BWGRKL, BWGRKN, and BWGRKI [Greek] PostScript® Type 1 and TrueType fonts Copyright © 1994–2013 BibleWorks, LLC. All rights reserved. These Biblical Greek and Hebrew fonts are used with permission and are from BibleWorks (www.bibleworks.com).

Scripture taken from the New American Standard Bible®, © Copyright 1960, 1962, 1963, 1968, 1971, 1972, 1973, 1975, 1977, 1995 by The Lockman Foundation. Used by permission. (www.Lockman.org)

Many Bible and scripture translations (DBY, GNT, NAB, NAS, NIV, KJV, YLT) come from BibleWorks™ Copyright © 1992–2001 Bible-Works LLC. All rights reserved.

Greek Bible text from: *The Greek New Testament,* Fourth revised edition, Edited by Barbara Aland and others, © 1993 Deutsche Bibelgesellschaft, Stuttgart.

www.ingramcontent.com/pod-product-compliance
Lightning Source LLC
Chambersburg PA
CBHW070427010526
44118CB00014B/1935